TIM CONNOR, CSP

SO-AEV-466

$You Call That ELLING

**Executive
Books**

You Call *That* Selling

Published by
Executive Books
206 West Allen Street
Mechanicsburg, PA 17055

Copyright © 2005 by Tim Connor

Cover Design by Gregory A. Dixon
Editor: Catherine Frenzel

ISBN: 1-933715-02-2

Printed in the United States of America

For information on Tim's services as a meeting or convention speaker, please call:
704-895-1230 ● 800-222-9070
or fax: 704-895-1231 ● 800-222-9071
Email: Tim@TimConnor.com
Website: www.TimConnor.com

A few of the best selling books by Tim Connor

Soft Sell
The Voyage
Sales Mastery
O.K. God, What's Next?
Lead, Manage or Get Out of the Way
The Trade-Off
You Call **THAT** Selling!
The Sales Handbook
How to Sell More In Less Time
The Ancient Scrolls
Life Questions
Crossroads—A Love Story
Peace of Mind
How to Be Happy AND Successful from A - Z
The Last Goodbye
Relationship Ruts and How to Avoid Them
52 Tips for Success, Wealth, and Happiness
Your First Year in Sales
That's Life!
Nit-pickers, Naggers & Tyrants
The Road to Happiness is Full of Potholes
The Male Gift-Giving Survival Guide

Contents

Have you met Seymour?

Sooner or later every salesperson meets Seymour. Actually he spells his name Seemore. He needs to see more and more and more. He never buys, but he needs to see more.

Are you spending too much time with a Seemore? Do you have a lot of Seemores in your territory?

How can you identify a Seemore quickly and easily? What can you do with him once you have identified him? And, how can you avoid him in the future?

Seemores come in all shades, ages, sexes, colors, and sizes. They do have one thing in common, however: They never buy. They waste a lot of your time and corporate resources, but they never give you an order. And be thankful they don't. If they did, they would still want to see more throughout the relationship. One way to quickly identify a Seemore is his interest in brochures, demonstrations, references – just lots of stuff. In some cases, a genuine prospect will want to see some of this, but a Seemore wants everything.

One way to treat a Seemore, when you begin to feel you are dealing with one, is to ask him a series of questions such as: In addition to all of this material I have provided you, what else will be necessary to get your business? When do you feel you will have enough information to make a buying decision? What is your decision process? What is your timing? You have to pin him down.

One way to avoid Seemores in the future is to be so busy and successful that you just don't have time for them. When they ask for lots of stuff initially, you can send it, but the next time they ask for more, come up with some reason not to accommodate them – i.e.: corporate policy, you are on the road, literature is being reprinted, etc. Ask them if this additional information is critical for a decision and why?

Seemores are everywhere. They take your time and energy and generally create stress and frustration in your career. They let you believe (and they often do a great job of convincing you) that they are serious prospects. Don't buy it. Sometimes the best policy is to walk away from them if you can.

Introduction

There are only two ways to sell more. Do less wrong or do more right. Imagine the results you could achieve if you did both?

This book will help you avoid many of the costly deal-breaking mistakes that thousands of salespeople make every day. It will also give you techniques or strategies to ensure that you eliminate these mistakes from your sales behaviors and replace them with proven approaches that, when used with confidence, skill, and consistency, will help you break your sales records year after year.

This book is not a sales manual for either beginners or seasoned veterans. It is, however, a straight-forward, no-holds-barred method for anyone in sales who wants to sell more in less time with less rejection and disappointment.

In my previous best sellers, *Soft Sell, Sales Mastery,* and *Your First Year in Sales,* I discuss a variety of concepts, principles, techniques, and attitudes that are required for success in selling. In this book, I cut to the chase and just give you the essence. One page for each common sales mistake or dumb thing that most salespeople do or say, sooner or later in their career.

They are listed by major topic area of the sales process. There are two ways to use or read this book. From beginning to end, learning and un-learning as you go. Or, you can go to the index and find the specific mistake that you think you are making and refer back to that page.

This is not a complicated process. However, I highly recommend that you record your thoughts on each topic in the journal section at the end of the book. If you run out of room, you can always buy a journal at Staples for a few bucks.

This journal section, over time, will become your most trusted resource for staying on top of the pile and avoiding sales slumps, disappointments, and lost sales. So, it is time to move on, since most sections are only one page and that includes this introduction. I will, however, scatter a number of thought-provoking quotes throughout the book for your pondering.

Sales Quiz

Write in or circle your answers before going any further (no peeking at the back of the book!).

1. One of the biggest mistakes salespeople make is ...

2. Attitude is important in sales because ...

3. Product features are what ...

4. Product customer benefits are ...

5. The close of the sale is ...

6. Sales objections are ...

7. Three of the most important sales skills are the ability to ...

8. The number one cause of failure in sales is ...

9. Rank the following in order of importance as they relate to sales success:

____ Product knowledge   ____ Prospect qualifying
____ Sales skills   ____ Closing techniques
____ Attitude management   ____ Presentation skills
____ People skills

10. People buy what or for what reasons?

11. People buy _____ and then justify their

    decision _____. Emotionally/logically

12. Your prospect will tell you ...

13. Rank the following in terms of most prospects' concerns:

    ____ Price   ____ Good terms
    ____ Quality   ____ Organization reputation
    ____ Service   ____ Product reliability
    ____ Convenience

14. The close of the sale should start ...

15. People like to buy, but don't like ...

16. What are your three best sources of new business?

17. The value of testimonials and references is ...

18. You can sell something you don't believe in. True/False

19. When is the best time to ask a customer for a referral?

20. If you have a good product, it will sell itself. True/False

21. The objection you will have the greatest difficulty overcoming is ...

22. You shouldn't ask for the order until you have covered all of the product features. True/False

23. Selling is an event, not a process. True/False

24. After-sales service can increase customer loyalty True/False

25. It is harder to sell on the telephone than in a personal sales call. True/False

26. Verbal messages are more accurate than non-verbal signals. True/False

27. The most important element of the sales process is …

28. Once you have lost business, it is difficult to regain it. True/False

29. Every prospect deserves equal selling time. True/False

30. Cold calling is the least/most effective way to prospect?

31. The Internet is making it easier/harder to sell?

32. The close of the sale is the end of the sales process. True/False

33. You can make up for a poor prospect with a good presentation and/or product. True/False

34. A planned presentation is more effective than a spontaneous customer-driven approach. True/False

35. It is better to ask more closed-ended questions than open-ended ones. True/False

36. If a prospect will see you, he/she is worth your time. True/False

37. You should make _____ number of calls on a prospect until he/she buys.

38. People buy from people they …

39. Sales records are important because …

40. The number one concern of most prospects is …

41. You can competitor-proof your relationship by …

42. If you are a good negotiator, you will close more sales. True/False

43. A prospect profile is an effective way to prospect because ...

44. Solving after-sales problems is considered good customer service. True/False

45. Planning your sales message should be done in your office/in the prospect's office?

46. Every sales presentation should have a certain amount of small-talk. True/False

47. When a prospect challenges your price, you should ...

48. Getting past the gate-keeper or voice-mail is one of the most difficult challenges of a salesperson. True/False

49. The two most important skills in selling are ...

50. Anyone can learn to sell. True /False

The biggest human temptation is to settle for too little.

Thomas Merton

Chapter One – Attitude Dumb Things

Attitudes. We all have them. Some contribute to your sales success while others sabotage your journey towards wealth, happiness, peace, and fulfillment. When was the last time you conducted a self-attitude audit? When was the last time you asked yourself, how are my attitudes shaping my present and future?

When was the last time you asked a customer, spouse, employee, supervisor, and/or friend how they feel about your attitudes? We build our days one attitude at a time. And over time we shape our lives one day at a time. Our destiny is nothing more than the daily accumulation of feelings and attitudes about ourselves, others, our past, present, and future.

Guard your attitudes and remember that we tend to become or think like what and who we are exposed to on a regular basis. Be careful of what you let into your inner world as well as who and what you let into your outer environment. Why not stop now and assess the people in your life and their impact on your attitudes. Why not stop right now and evaluate where you need to make changes in thoughts, perceptions, interpretations, and/or beliefs.

There is no right or wrong. The real question is: Are your attitudes helping you move more smoothly and successfully along the path of life?

In this first chapter we will cover many of the common attitude mistakes that salespeople tend to make that sabotage their career success. Yes, there are many that are not covered, but my guess is that if you can avoid many or all of them, you will be well on your way to setting sales records and financial independence.

Don't go around saying the world owes you a living. The world owes you nothing. It was here first.

Mark Twain

> ### Dumb Thing #1
> ### Lacking clear focus.

You usually bring into your life whatever is consistent with your focus. You can focus either on what is not working or what is, what you don't have or you do, what you want or what you don't, what you believe in or don't. There is a great line (can't remember where I heard it; just know I am not taking credit for it) that says, be careful what you ask for, you might just get it.

One of my favorite quotes is by Arthur Ashe. He said, "True greatness is, start where you are, use what you have and do what you can."

Most sales winners in life are grateful for their blessings, focus on what they want, have, and can do. By the same token, most losers focus on what is missing, where they are not, and on what they can't do.

Let me give you an example:

Salesperson A complains constantly about: prices are too high, brochures are not up to date, they don't have laptops or cellular phones, their territory is too small and has too few good prospects, there is inadequate internal support staff, it's raining.... You get the picture: If they are doing poorly, they can find a reason why (other than themselves).

Salesperson B – winners – on the other hand, learn to work with what they have. They improvise, innovate, adjust, compromise – whatever it takes to get the job done with the tools they have. A key ingredient in all leaders, winners, effective people, and productive and/or successful organizations is focus.

> ### Smart Thing #1
> ### Focus on what you want, not what you don't want.

> **Dumb Thing #2**
>
> **Stop learning.**

Is next year going to be better than last year or about the same or worse?

Every year thousands of salespeople start the New Year with big goals, wonderful intentions, and executable plans. However, at the end of each year, thousands of salespeople can be heard asking themselves, "Where did I miss the boat? What did I miss? Why was this year not much better than last year?"

Over the years, one common denominator I have observed in successful salespeople is their willingness to invest in the continued improvement of their skills, attitudes, and philosophy.

What did you invest last year in yourself? Not in your bank balance, home improvements, travel, or daily maintenance. And you don't get to include what your company invested on your behalf in seminars, courses, or learning materials. If you are excelling in this demanding career, I will guarantee you have invested more in yourself than you have in going out to dinner. If you have invested more in personal entertainment, I will bet you are not achieving what you could and that you end each month or year with frustration and worry.

Life is an interesting relationship between paying the price and winning the prize. Between self-investment and rewards. Between investing time in personal development and your ultimate success. It is never too late to begin an aggressive on-going self development program. There are hundreds of books to read, audio albums to listen to, and seminars to attend. Don't wait for your organization to invest in you and your future value. Take full responsibility for the quality of your life and learning, and I strongly urge you to DO IT NOW.

> **Smart Thing #2**
>
> **Invest 10% of your time and money in self-improvement.**

> **Dumb Thing #3**
> **Not being organized.**

Clutter. Technology. Stuff. A full plate. Sales reports. Personal interests. Home life. Career. Relatives. Friends. Too little time. Too much to do. Meetings. The list goes on and on and on.

One of the things I have discovered about successful salespeople is their ability to handle a variety of tasks, problems, issues, responsibilities, and challenges at the same time. I am talking here about personal management.

Personal management means:

1. Start with a plan of what you want to do.
2. Prioritize your goals, objectives, tasks, projects – whatever.
3. Stay focused.
4. Get rid of the clutter in your life.
5. Concentrate on one thing at a time.
6. Don't stick with anything that you are not passionate about.
7. Have routines for the regular tasks in your life.
8. Get up earlier. Go to bed later.
9. Organize your workspace so that you can be more productive.
10. Learn to say *no* more often.
11. Develop the habit of Doing It Now.
12. Don't make commitments you can't keep.
13. Respect and value your own time.
14. Play when it is time to play and work when it is time to work.
15. Use technology as a tool, not a crutch.
16. Throw stuff away you don't need, use, or want.

> **Smart Thing #3**
> **Plan everything. Finish it.**
> **Then move on to the next thing.**

Dumb Thing #4
Lacking clear purpose.

Loss of purpose in sales is akin to loss of faith or patience in your ability to perform effectively and successfully. It is a feeling that no matter what you do, it will not be good enough or soon enough. It is nagging questions that keep popping into your consciousness.

Purpose is the single most important motivator in a salesperson's life. It keeps you keeping on when all around you is caving in before your eyes – a time when nothing seems to work, when people have abandoned you, and life seems to have forgotten that you exist.

There is no easy way to regain your purpose. It is a function of many elements such as: will, desire, resolve, faith, and trust. The way to discover or re-discover your purpose takes time, effort, passion, patience, contemplation, self-evaluation, and commitment. These traits are not inborn or easily acquired, but in the end, once you own them, there is nothing that can stand in your way as you move into the rest of your sales career and life.

The first step in discovering (or re-discovering) your purpose is to find what you love, what you are passionate about, and why you are in a sales career in the first place. Most people live their lives always hoping for something better, but they refuse or don't know how to do the work on themselves necessary to discover their purpose. I didn't discover mine until my late 30's after devouring dozens of sales and self-help books and contemplating hundreds of questions. Finally, it came to me after more hours than I care to admit in laborious and often difficult self-appraisal: "I want to help people with what I have learned on my life's journey." This led to my speaking and training and, eventually, my writing.

Smart Thing #4
Decide what is important in your life and never let it go.

> ### Dumb Thing #5
> ### Losing your excitement.

Passion is the great equalizer. It can make up for a lack of experience and knowledge. I am not suggesting that you not develop your knowledge or experience, however, because they will only enhance and further empower your passion – your strong belief in yourself, your mission, and your purpose.

Passion is different than enthusiasm. The old cliché says, "Act enthusiastic and you will become enthusiastic." I have never subscribed to this philosophy. Why? Because if enthusiasm is an act that you use when things are going well, how do you behave when your life is falling apart? Are you just as enthusiastic about failure, about more problems than you deserve, and any number of disappointments, frustrations, and adversities?

Passion is not an act. It is a way of believing. It is woven into your cellular structure just as much as your DNA. Passion, real passion for who you are, who you are becoming, where you are, and where you are going, what you believe in, stand for, and would die for shouts to the world, "I am here to stay, I am here to make a difference, I will leave my mark in this world. It may take me my entire life, but I will not give up until my purpose and destiny are realized." Who do you know that is passionate about something? Anything?

You can see it in their eyes, hear it in their voice, and sense it in their behavior. How are you doing? Are you in love with where you are, where you are going, who you are becoming, and what you are contributing? Or are you living like over 85% of the population with the attitude, "Same Stuff, Different Day."

If you have lost or are losing your passion for your sales career, do whatever is necessary to get it back.

> ### Smart Thing #5
> ### Keep the passion alive in your career and life.

> ### Dumb Thing #6
> ## Quitting too soon.

You would be amazed at how many people quit just before they are about to achieve the success they have been working toward. They just get tired of waiting, trying, or dreaming and give up. Why is this?

I believe it is for one of six reasons:

1. They really didn't want what they were going after in the first place.
2. They thought it would be easier.
3. They thought it would come sooner, rather than later.
4. They lost belief in themselves or their mission or cause.
5. They let someone else discourage them or talk them out of wanting it.
6. They failed to realize that anything worthwhile takes time, faith, patience – and yes, action.

Is there an area in your life today where you are wavering? Thinking about giving up? I have been there. I know what it feels like to want to quit. But in the end, I realized I didn't really want to quit. I just felt sorry for myself. Not a pretty picture.

No one can determine another person's limits of endurance or courage. No one can judge what another person is willing or not willing to do. Never let anyone talk you out of your dream, no matter how well meaning they might appear.

Go for it. Keep at it. Just do it and enjoy the process. Don't expect there will always be a crowd cheering you on. Much of success is enjoyed in quiet solitude, one moment at a time.

> ### Smart Thing #6
> ## Never give up, never. No matter how hard it gets.

Dumb Thing #7
Giving in to self-imposed limitations.

It has been said by many people smarter than me that "the only limitations we encounter in life are those self-limiting ones we place on ourselves." If this is true, and at this point I am neither agreeing nor disagreeing with this premise, why then do so few people reach their full potential? Why do so many people feel stuck, out of control, and without hope in their lives? Why do so many people give up, quit, settle, resign themselves, or operate out of blame, anger, guilt, resentment, and self pity when it comes to the quality of their life? If this question were answered in a book by the same title, it would never sell. Why? Because the very people we are talking about here do not want to take responsibility for their lives. They insist on pointing their finger toward something or someone else for the cause of their station or circumstances in life.

Each of us came into this world headed for greatness in some way. We were engineered for success at birth and conditioned for failure along the way. There is nothing we cannot do if we put our mind and all of our energy and passion into it. The skeptics out there are thinking, "Sure Tim, I can fly."

I do not have the time or the interest to deal with skeptics or critics if that is their attitude. Certainly there are some physical limitations in some areas or with some people. My only point here is that most of us could do more if we would only learn that most of our ceilings are self-imposed.

What inner mental images are you holding in your consciousness that may be holding you back? Is it the fear of failure or success? Is it the fear of rejection or public scorn? Is it an inner feeling of unworthiness? Or is it some other emotional issue or scar that you have failed to recognize or deal with?

Smart Thing #7
You can do whatever you put your mind and energy to.

Dumb Thing #8
Seeing failure as negative.

If you are failing at something, great. You can learn more when things are going badly than when they are working. If you are not failing, you are not stretching.

Is failure positive or negative? It depends. One person can experience a result, outcome, or consequence and give up while another person can experience the same issue and use it to get better, stronger, wiser, or any other positive response.

No one escapes this life without failures. I have had them. You have had them. Everyone has had them. The only way to avoid failure is to spend the rest of your life in some log cabin in the woods away from all human contact, expectations, and the need for achievement. I know of no one who has reached adulthood who has not had some form of adversity or failure in their life. Neither do you. Why then are we so afraid to fail? If I was worried or offended by those rejections, I certainly would not be working on my 10th and 11th books.

So go out there and fail. Push. Try. You have nothing to lose and everything to gain. All success requires you to be tested on the anvils of time, adversity, problems, and life itself.

I know no one who has achieved great success who has not had their share of failures. Get in the habit of measuring your success, not by what you have achieved, but by how many times you have failed and come back again.

Smart Thing #8
Fail often so you can succeed sooner.

> **Dumb Thing #9**
> **Trying to do it all by yourself.**

There is a wonderful way to cut 20 years off the learning curve in your career. It is to hang out with people who are where you want to be or people who have done what you want to do. The key is to create a win/win relationship. A mentor is one of many ways to accomplish this objective.

What is a mentor? It is a person who is interested in your success, happiness, well-being, or future, and wants to make a contribution. These people don't necessarily have to be in the same business, have the same interests, or have been successful in their chosen field. What a mentor brings to the mentor/mentee relationship is insight, feedback, integrity, a willingness to help, and genuine concern for the mentee.

The mentor always gains something in this relationship, but it isn't always apparent what. You don't need hundreds of mentors. One can accelerate your career, two can skyrocket it, three can keep you learning and growing nonstop. I suggest you look through your contacts and see if you can find someone who can contribute to your career success and ask them to meet with you. If the person is a thousand miles away, just call them. Everybody has a phone.

The key to a successful mentor/mentee relationship is setting the ground rules up front as to each person's role, expectations, agendas, time use, accountability, and feedback. The right mentor(s) can save you time, energy, and money. They can challenge your thinking, hold you accountable, help you reach your goals, and have fun in the process.

Find someone who can help you. Take advantage of their insight, experience, and knowledge.

> **Smart Thing #9**
> **Have mentors and a personal coach.**

> **Dumb Thing #10**
> **Lacking gratitude.**

Have you ever noticed that some people seem to have more of some things – or everything – than others? More fun, stuff, friends, success, money, influence, achievements, wisdom, peace, harmony, freedom – just to mention a few.

Why is this? Over the years, I have observed hundreds of people in all walks of life, especially salespeople. As a speaker, I am privileged to meet thousands of people each year in my programs. One thing I have seen is a wide-ranging array of attitudes, feelings, and beliefs. It is interesting to note that the people I have met who have the greatest degree of peace, joy, harmony, life balance, friends, and success (no matter how you choose to define success) are people who live with a great deal of gratitude in their lives.

Some of you might believe that you have nothing to be grateful for. Life is just – same stuff different day, or just a bowl of pits, or not fair, or whatever. Here are a few things we have to be grateful for that many people take for granted:

1. Air to breathe and food to eat.
2. Bodies that work and minds that can think.
3. Books to read.
4. People who care about you.
5. Hearts that pump 2,500,000 a month.
6. Work that is satisfying, challenging, or contributes to our growth

Refer to this list often. Refer to it when you are feeling sorry for yourself, when you have failed, been let down, lost your way, feel like quitting, feel good, feel bad, when you are sick, and when you are healthy.

> **Smart Thing #10**
> **Feel and show gratitude for everything.**

> ### Dumb Thing #11
> ### Being pessimistic.

Is the glass half full or half empty? Will this product, policy, or strategy work or fail? Can I really achieve my dreams or am I living in fantasyland? These and hundreds of questions are asked every day by well-meaning and hard-working salespeople.

Lionel Tiger in his great book *Optimism, The Biology of Hope*, written over 40 years ago, discusses how optimism impacts a person's attitudes, outlook, success, and health. He suggests that people who are less optimistic about life, the present, and the future tend to get sick more frequently and often die sooner. In his book *Learned Optimism,* Martin Segilman discusses how each of us begins every project, activity, task, relationship, career, etc., with either a YES or a NO – a YES, I-can-and-I-will or NO, I-can't-and-I-won't – in our heart.

You can't measure optimism. You can't bottle it, regulate it, run out of it, or manufacture it, but you can learn to develop it if you will only take the time and effort. Some people feel it is better to be realistic than optimistic – why set yourself up for disappointment? Tell me what is realistic? Looking back over the past 100 years, where would we be if Edison, Bell, Gates, Ford, Land, Disney, et. al., were realistic? If their attitude had been: It hasn't been done yet, so I guess it can't be done!

There are numerous benefits to having an optimistic outlook. And just as many pitfalls in not having one.

Here are a few of the benefits: You will achieve more, you will have more fun. You will be happier, you will have more friends, you will enjoy life more, and you will be healthier.

> ### Smart Thing #11
> ### You have nothing to lose by being optimistic.

Dumb Thing #12

Not improving your self-esteem.

When you look in the mirror, listen to your own voice on a recording device, see yourself in a photo or on a video screen, is your first reaction:

- I could like myself better if…?
- I will like myself better when…?
- I'm really OK just the way I am?

When you fail, is your first reaction:

- To blame others or circumstances?
- Take full responsibility for your own life outcomes?
- Begin again?
- Never try again?

When life gives you a problem, do you:

- Look for an excuse or scapegoat?
- Adjust?
- Quit?

When someone says unpleasant things about you, do you:

- Get angry at them?
- Accept their view as theirs and in no way related to who you are?

When you receive a compliment, do you:

- Make excuses?
- Thank them?

When you succeed, do you:

- Pat yourself on the back?
- Belittle your success?

Smart Thing #12

Find ways to like yourself more every day.

> **Dumb Thing #13**
> **Not believing in yourself.**

Do you believe in, trust, and accept yourself? This is one of the keys to success and happiness.

Belief in oneself is the knowledge that no matter what crosses your path, you can handle it. No matter how hard you fall, how long you are down, or who is kicking you while you are down, this too will pass and you can learn from the experience.

There are two types of people in the world. Those who whine and those who act. Those who believe in a better tomorrow and those who don't. Those who blame and those who take responsibility. Those who resist the pull of life into the future and those who flow with it.

Self-belief says: Throw it at me, life; I will handle it, overcome it, and I will survive and succeed.

A lack of self-belief says: I quit, I can't do it, it's too much for me.

What is your approach to adversity, trouble, failure, problems, challenges, or any negative circumstances? Do you have a YES or NO in your heart?

As you begin each new day, are you poised to GO FOR IT? To tackle whatever life throws in your path? To never give in or give up?

We won't do it ALL, have it ALL, learn it ALL in life. It just isn't that kind of world. But you have nothing to lose and a great deal to gain by pushing the edges and your limits. Trust the process of your life and the opportunities that cross your path and give it all you've got.

> **Smart Thing #13**
> **Believe in yourself even when no one else does.**

Dumb Thing #14

Lacking integrity.

Integrity and trust go hand in hand as qualities for sales success. It is not possible to have one without the other. If you trust someone, it is most likely because they are trustworthy and they have ethics (or integrity). If a person lacks either of the two, they generally will lack both.

It is the willingness and ability to do what IS right – not what you or others *think* is right – and there is often a difference. Most people who have been brought up in the right surroundings know what IS right, yet they hope they can get away with something – anything – and that their words and/or actions will remain forever locked in their own mind.

The question we must ask ourselves when we consider doing what IS NOT right vs. what IS, is: Can I handle getting caught? Is the price worth it? How will I react to getting caught? Wouldn't it just be easier to deal in truth? All the time? The answer is YES. So why do people misrepresent, lie, tell little innocent fibs, etc.? I don't know. We are all guilty – at least one time in our lives and most of us several times – of shading the truth for what we feel is a justifiable cause. Is this wrong? I am not a moralist. But I do believe that character and integrity are related.

Here are a few simple questions to ask the next time you are considering anything less than truth:

1. What will I lose and gain by dealing in un-truth?
2. Who will this lack of truth impact other than me?
3. Is it easy for me to shade the truth, and do I do it often? Why?
4. If I deal only in the truth – all the time – what will that do for me?

Smart Thing #14

Always deal in the truth, no matter what.

> **Dumb Thing #15**
>
> **Getting discouraged.**

Have you ever wanted to quit? Anything? What is the cause of discouragement? Is it a sense of loss? Feeling out of control? Loss of faith in yourself or the future? Is it feeling that your present circumstances will never end? I can only tell you that this emotion, more than most other emotions, will drain your creativity, purpose, and resolve.

Discouragement is a signal that something is wrong, something in your life needs to change. You can pay attention to its warning signs and find another way to approach whatever is causing your pain – or you can choose to whine, blame, or hide.

The one thing which has helped me more than any other is my faith in God and the knowledge that "this, too, would pass." I have known deep in my soul and heart that what was happening was necessary for me in order to make a change in my life. It was life's way of guiding me to a better tomorrow. It was not meant to break me, but to show me a better path. For many years, I ignored this inner guidance, feeling that I could do everything on my own without help from anyone or anywhere. As I matured, however, I came to learn and accept that we all need help from somewhere or someone sooner or later.

People will often let you down in your time of need. There is one guiding truth we all must learn if we are to overcome the feelings of loss of control: We are all on God's path to perfection, and we will all make mistakes traveling that path.

If you are discouraged today about anything, know that this discouragement is in your life for your higher good. I know that while you are in the depths of despair this is a difficult request, but it is one that I believe you must learn to accept with grace and gratitude.

> **Smart Thing #15**
>
> **Remember that all things pass. Just relax.**

> **Dumb Thing #16**
> **Lacking self-discipline.**

In life, we either pay the price of discipline or the price of regret. We pay these prices in all areas of our life: our careers, relationships, health, spiritual development, and financial affairs. It is unfortunate that many of us, yours truly included, fail to comprehend this simple law of life.

Let me explain. The laws that apply to all of life's issues such as discipline, commitment, patience, integrity, practice, self-control, and focus either help us live with freedom, peace, and harmony or heartache, failure, regrets, and misfortune as we move along the path of life. Much of the latter could be avoided (not all of it) if we would understand, accept, and integrate this simple truth into our lives.

The price of discipline is that daily dose of exercise, that moderation in our life affairs, our eating habits, our relationship strategies such as open and honest communication, and managing our resources wisely. The lack of these daily little disciplines accumulates day by day and year by year until each of us inherits the consequences of these misdeeds.

I have had many personal experiences where the daily lack of discipline one day came back and haunted me. I am discovering through these learning experiences that no one is immune to this truth. Arrogance, ignorance, or a combination of both is no excuse, and life really doesn't give a twit if you claim either. We pay one way or another. And discipline weighs ounces, while regret weighs tons.

The pain of discipline is nothing compared to the sting of regret.

> **Smart Thing #16**
> **Remember, it is better to pay the price**
> **of discipline than regret.**

> **Dumb Thing #17**
> **Trying to be someone else.**

Being – who you are – is often a very difficult task. Managers, customers, spouses, friends, parents, and siblings often ask us directly or indirectly to behave in ways that are consistent with who *they* think we should be. For many years I have been accused of being a maverick. That word can mean many different things to each of us. I don't know whether I am or not, but I do know that we can't be happy, successful, or at peace with ourselves or the world as long as we are being anyone other than who we are. Yes, we are developing, growing, changing, and becoming, but all of this needs to be according to our own inner drive to be.

When we allow others to determine who we should be, how we should behave, what we should believe, how we should feel – I know, I know, a lot of shoulds – but that is precisely the point. Who SHOULD determine who we are? This is not rocket science, my friends. It is really quite simple: As long as you let others determine your destiny, personality, behavior, feelings, etc., you will never be really happy or successful (no matter how you choose to define success) nor will you ever be at peace with yourself.

Who in your life is not happy with who you are or who you are becoming? How are they attempting to influence your evolution?

Don't let them do it. I have done so many times in the past. I have caved in and have always regretted it. I am not saying, don't change. I am only suggesting that when you change, change when you are ready for a new you, for whatever reason.

Being true to yourself – to your values, dreams, hopes, desires, needs, and so on – is one of the greatest gifts you can give to yourself and the rest of the world.

> **Smart Thing #17**
> **Grow and change on your own terms,**
> **not those of others.**

Dumb Thing #18

Lacking honest intent.

Intent is important, but your success comes from your action – what you do. I believe it is important to have positive (good) intentions, but show me what a person *does*, and I will show you what their *real* intent was.

- I know people who consistently say: "Some day I will…."
- I have heard hundreds of times: "I would like to start my own business, but…."
- I have observed thousands of people say they want to lose weight, but can't give up that last french-fry or piece of carrot cake.
- I have heard hundreds of commitments from people who said they would – call me back, meet me at noon for lunch, send me something, etc., etc. – and never heard a word or saw them again.

I will bet you have had many of the same experiences. The real question is: Are you guilty of any of them? I have been, many times. I said for years I wanted to lose weight and kept eating and eating myself into oblivion. Said I wanted to write a book for over five years before I wrote *Soft Sell* in 1981. By the way, its sales are now over 500,000 copies worldwide and still going strong.

A few questions for you:

1. Is your word your bond?
2. Do you make promises to pacify people?
3. Do you do what you say you will do?
4. Do you let little roadblocks keep you from taking positive action?
5. Do you vacillate on what you want to do and why?
6. Do you talk about doing things to see how other people will react?
7. Do you talk about doing something to convince yourself?

Smart Thing #18

Do what you say you are going to do.

> **Dumb Thing #19**
>
> **Letting your life slip by.**

There are a number of outstanding reasons to keep a journal. Let's name a few of them. They are easy to write, don't take up lots of space, and they will stimulate your thoughts and help you remember important experiences and events. A journal can:

1. Help you avoid drastic errors in judgment
2. Increase your effectiveness
3. Improve your income
4. Help you learn from your failures
5. Improve your relationships
6. Help you achieve your goals
7. Keep you headed in the right direction
8. Improve your lifestyle
9. Help you learn from others
10. Help you find peace and happiness
11. Save you time
12. Help you have more fun
13. Capture valuable memories

If this isn't enough to get you to consider starting and keeping a personal success journal, I don't know what will. I can only tell you from personal experience that keeping a record of my insights, thoughts, ideas, successes, mistakes, errors, achievements and failures, and their causes, has done more for my career than any other single activity.

What have you got to lose? It takes less than ten minutes a day to capture all of those important little day-by-day events, feelings, activities, and their consequences that, when re-visited on a regular basis, can have a galvanizing impact on your career, relationships, and life.

> **Smart Thing #19**
>
> **Start and keep a journal for your career success.**

Dumb Thing #20
Being out of balance.

One of the issues facing many people today is the ability to maintain a sense of balance in their lives. It is impossible to have *total* balance in your life. There are too many demands, issues, problems, needs, goals, and people to deal with. It *is* possible, however, to have enough balance to reduce the stress in your life while enjoying many of the gifts life has to offer.

Several areas that we need to balance are: family, work, finances, friends, social relationships, spirituality, self-development, physical well-being, personal interests, business or career interests, and fun. At any given time, you can be way out of balance – e.g., if you have just started a new business or career, you have just had your first child, or you are in a new relationship. It is normal to devote more time and energy to these activities while ignoring some of the others. The problem arises if we stay out of balance in one area for a long period of time – e.g., working 7 days a week for 25 years at the expense of your health, friends, and family.

What are some steps we can take if we are out of balance?

1. Spend time deciding what is really important in your life, both short and long term.
2. Share your goals, dreams, needs, and frustrations about being out of balance with the people in your life that matter.
3. Learn to set better priorities.
4. Say *no* more often.
5. Determine where you are out of balance and ask yourself, why.
6. Spend time better planning your days, weeks, months, and years.
7. Get up an hour earlier or go to bed an hour later.
8. Accept the fact that there are times in your life when you will be temporarily out of balance.
9. Simplify your life.

Smart Thing #20
Live the balanced life you want to live.

Dumb Thing #21
Lacking patience.

Patience is a virtue. Sure, that's easy to say while you are waiting for a plane to take off that is three hours late, or a friend you are meeting for lunch is 30 minutes late, or life happens the way you feel it should according to your personal schedule. One lesson life will teach you is the need for patience in *all* things – from the behavior of your customers to the traffic on the way to an appointment. Why not look at patience from a few different perspectives?

1. Patience is really testing your faith.
2. Patience is really testing your resolve.
3. Patience is testing your level of trust.
4. Patience is testing your level of understanding.
5. Patience is testing your degree of acceptance.

Each of us is faced daily with people, circumstances, issues, and "life" that gets in our face and says, "What are you made of?" Each of us responds differently to these challenges when they appear. Some people cave in, while others strive on. Some get stronger, while others give up. Some people learn, while others point their finger elsewhere as the cause of their misfortune. Some people take responsibility for the quality of their life, while others see themselves as victims. Some people whine, while others get on with it.

Patience can be seen on the faces of people who do not let life's stressors send them ballistic. These people flow with life: the good, the bad, and the ugly. They realize that life is a mix of all of this, and lacking patience is to expect life and everything in it to be perfect – all the time. Well, my friends, welcome to the real world – a world with imperfections, struggle, pain, success, failure, problems, achievements, old age, and anything else positive or negative you can think of.

Smart Thing #21
Relax and enjoy the ride. Anything less could kill you.

Dumb Thing #22

Letting sales slumps get you down.

Every salesperson experiences a slump sometime in their career.

Let's first define what I call a sales slump. Perhaps you think that the only sign of a slump is a period of reduced sales success, regardless of its nature or length. It is not quite that simple. There are a number of ways a salesperson can be in a slump. Any salesperson, regardless of experience or length of service, can find themselves having a difficult time with one or more of the sales process issues or elements addressed in this book. They are:

1. Controlling your attitudes
2. Effective prospecting
3. Tailored presentations
4. Asking for the business and
5. After-sales service

Successful salespeople know that selling is a process and not an event. They have learned that their role is to create relationships that lead to sales. It is not just moving products off the floor.

The key to long-term success for any salesperson is to manage all of the five elements in a consistent and positive way. What good does it do in the long run to have great closing skills if you are never in the presence of good prospects? What good does it do to have excellent products and services if you can't get appointments? What good does it do to have a good prospect if you can't ask for the business? Notice, I didn't say, "Ask for the *order*" – but, for the *business*.

You can experience a sales slump in any one of these areas. Regardless of the issue, the results will generally be the same. Low sales. Low margins. Lost customers. Vulnerable to competition. Selling price to get the business, and so on.

If you are experiencing a slump, you can't just look at the big picture. You must look carefully at your approach, strategies, strengths, and weaknesses in each of the five categories. You must learn to ask yourself the right questions, if you hope to get accurate information that will help you out of this negative sales period. Knowing the characteristics or causes that contributed to the current situation will also help you prevent future slumps.

Smart Thing #22
Recognize that there will always be ups and downs in your career.

> **Dumb Thing #23**
> **Lacking clear goals.**

There is one major reason for setting goals: Goals give your life direction. Daily direction, weekly direction, and yearly direction.

Don't be attached to the outcomes – only the process. One example. Diets. The key to weighing your ideal weight is not to take in more than you can burn off. That's it, folks. Eating carrot cake every night and not exercising is moving in the wrong direction. Guess what? You can't reach your ideal goal (weight) if you travel in the wrong direction.

What direction are you moving in as you travel down the highways of your life? There are seven highways that we are all on. They are: a financial highway, a family highway, a spiritual highway, a mental highway, a career highway, a social highway, and a physical highway. One of the biggest mistakes most people make as they travel into their future via each of these highways is to sacrifice one for another. Or to not understand that avoiding one of the areas will cause an interruption in all of them at some point in the future.

There are seminars, books, tapes, videos, and courses on how to, why to, when to, etc., set goals. Some say write them down, some say commit them to memory. I am not going to take issue with any of these authors or speakers. I only ask you to consider one simple concept: Are you moving daily in the direction that – if followed for several years – will land you where you want to be, if life gives you enough time? If you are not, change course today. NOW. Our lives are nothing more than the accumulation of moments, days, weeks, and years. Destiny is the result of all of this daily stuff, so pay attention to it.

> **Smart Thing #23**
> **Spend routine time in goal-setting activities.**

Dumb Thing #24

Letting your ego get in the way.

The ego wants to make you look good, keep you in control, and manipulate people, events, and life. It needs for you to be right. You need to control your ego, if you want to be happy and successful.

People whose lives are ruled by their egos tend to be filled with conflict, anxiety, stress, frustration, disappointment, and emotional game playing.

Blame, resentment, anger, fear, and guilt, are just a few of the emotional tools these people use. They are rarely ever truly happy. Oh yes, they might have fame, power, wealth, good looks, lots of toys, but most secretly know they are not really happy. Now there are many people who have these achievements and do enjoy a happy existance, but it is not because of these. They would be just as happy if they lost any or all of them.

One way to see if your ego is out of control is to look at how much conflict, disappointment, and stress you have in your life. These are often good indicators of who is in charge, your ego or your heart. Your heart wants only to be happy, your mind wants you to be right.

One of the biggest problems for many people is making the 18-inch journey from living their life from their heart rather than from their mind. How are you doing?

Smart Thing #24

Keep your ego out of the sales process.

Dumb Thing #25

Not managing your stress.

Stress in life is normal. Everything causes stress. There are positive things like promotions, marriage, relocation, starting a business, winning the lottery, retirement, having a baby, and any number of such things that cause stress. There are also negative things such as failure, getting fired, divorce, missing a deadline, having a baby, getting promoted, starting a business, winning the lottery, death of a loved one, relocating, etc., etc., etc. Did you notice that I repeated some of the items in each list? Not a mistake, folks; it was intentional. Stress is not about what is happening, but how you respond to those things.

Stressors are not positive or negative. A re-location can be positive for one person and negative for another. A promotion can do the same, and so can all of the others I mentioned, as well as all the ones I didn't. How can the death of a loved one be interpreted as a positive stressor? Personally, I don't know of anyone who wishes for the death of a loved one. But I am confident that somewhere out there in this world there is someone who will be relieved when a sick relative finally passes away, and that they no longer have to deal with the pain and humiliation that sometimes disease can bring.

Stress is not caused by events. If it were, everyone would have the same reaction or response to similar events, and we know that this isn't true. Stress can kill you or keep you alive. Stress can and will destroy your happiness if you do not learn to accept the reality of life and all of its issues, stuff, problems, and challenges. The key to successfully managing the stressors in your life is to develop some practical routines that help reduce the impact of these on your emotional and physical well-being. Things like exercise, prayer, meditation, laughter, fun, new routines, etc.

Smart Thing #25

Recognize that your reaction to stress is entirely up to you.

> **Dumb Thing #26**
> **Lacking confidence in yourself.**

If there is one character trait that stands above all the rest when it comes to increased success, it would be self-confidence. Granted, when we begin to list all of the traits necessary for success, we could fill a book. From Attitude to Zeal and everything in between. Some are more important than others. Integrity certainly must be included, along with persistence, belief, resilience, and resolve.

We could list all of them, but I would like to focus on self-confidence. Self-confidence gives you the ability to:

- Overcome obstacles
- Deal with rejection
- Overcome failure
- Deal with adversity
- Take risks

People who have a high degree of self-confidence can often be perceived as being arrogant, cocky, aloof, insensitive, and conceited – but these traits do not *have to* accompany self-confidence. People with some of the negative traits don't necessarily possess self-confidence. If you *are* self-confident, what can you do? Be careful that it does not lead you into the trap of developing the negative traits mentioned above. If you *lack* self-confidence, what can you do?

1. Determine in what circumstances you lack confidence.
2. Find areas where you can act confidently and build on those.
3. Ask a simple question: What am I afraid of when I lack confidence?
4. Take small steps in the beginning of a new activity, project, etc. You don't have to tackle the world in one bite.

> **Smart Thing #26**
> **Improve yourself every day.**

Dumb Thing #27
Living outside-in.

Living inside-out means taking the responsibility for the quality of your life; i.e., its successes, failures, achievements, outcomes, risks, happiness, financial position, lifestyle, relationships, etc. People who live outside-in turn the responsibility for their happiness, success, failures, etc., over to someone or something outside of themselves. They blame the weather, government, spouse, the economy, their company or organization, where they live, their parents – the list goes on and on.

We are in a crisis of responsibility in many parts of the world today. No one wants to take the responsibility for burning themselves with hot coffee, getting fired, going broke, experiencing a divorce. Everyone seems to want to point the finger elsewhere.

One of the discoveries I have made during the past 40 years is that people who live inside-out have more, do more, are happier, are more productive, are more successful, and are more balanced than people who live outside-in. This doesn't mean that inside-out people live carefree lives without adversity, problems, risks, failures, and a variety of negative issues. What they do differently is understand their role in the outcomes of their lives.

How are you doing today? Are you living from the inside-out or the outside-in? All you have to do to find out, if you don't know, is pay attention to how you react to the bumps, curves, disappointments, and people in your life that bring bad news, negative stuff, or issues that you feel you shouldn't have in your life. Inside-out people get just as many flat tires as outside-in people do, but watch the reaction and you can quickly tell who is who, even if it is you.

Smart Thing #27
Live inside-out.

Dumb Thing #28

Not managing expectations.

One of life's biggest frustrations is the unrealized expectations of other people's behavior. Why won't the people in my life act the way I think they should? They never will, so relax and let it go. You can never be happy attached to the expectations or outcomes you have for other people, no matter who they are.

The execution of all behavior by others is in their hands, not yours. I am not implying here that you should never have expectations, but that if you want to spend a lot of time and energy being disappointed, expect others to do whatever you believe, feel, or think they should – according to *your* standards. Sooner or later everyone – yes, everyone – will let you down. That's not being negative, just realistic.

Managing your expectations means you understand that everyone is doing the best they can with what they have learned thus far in life. We are all learning every day, either by accident, design, or on purpose. We are learning what life wants us to learn about life, relationships, people, business, and so on – now. Please keep in mind that people are not setting out deliberately to disappoint you, upset you, make you miserable, make you angry, fearful, or whatever; they are just being themselves. You have no right to expect another person to live their life according to how you believe they should. Yes, you can hope, ask, beg, and rant and rave until you are blue in the face, but, in the end, people are who they are, believe what they believe, feel what they feel, and act consistently with all of these.

Managing expectations also requires that we learn to love others as they grow through the individual lessons that life has thrown in their path, in spite of our attitudes, feelings, or beliefs. They may not always act as we would have, or we think they should have, but guess what? That's OK. A question: Do you want to live your life according to others' expectations? I didn't think so!

Smart Thing #28

Let go of illusions.

Dumb Thing #29

Repeating the same mistakes.

One of my heroes, Ben Franklin, who was one of the great minds of his generation over 250 years ago, had a simple program for success, wealth, and happiness. As one of the people who shaped the United States in the 1700's, he put forward the following approach to achieve success in any area of your life. I felt so strongly about these virtues that I put them in Chapter One of my best-seller *Soft Sell* over 20 years ago. I have not changed my mind. You might feel that one or more no longer applies in today's world; however, if that is your feeling, I would ask that you not discard his message too quickly, but look just a little deeper into your belief system for your reasons.

What Franklin proposed was to take a total of 13 virtues and live with each of them for one week at a time, integrating it, applying it, thinking about it, and making it a part of your consciousness. At the beginning of the second week you would move on to the next one, repeating the process. When you completed the 13th virtue, you would go back and begin the process again. The result is that during the course of a year, you will spend four weeks living and breathing each of the 13 virtues. At the beginning of the next year you repeat the process again. You can't imagine the power of repetition and what it can do for your attitudes, behavior, and overall well-being. Here are his 13 virtues:

1. **Temperance** – Eat not to dullness, drink not to elevation.
2. **Silence** – Speak not but what may benefit others or yourself.
3. **Order** – Let all your things have their places. Let each part of your business have its time.
4. **Resolution** – Resolve to perform what you ought. Perform without fail what you resolve.
5. **Frugality** – Make not expense but to do good to others or yourself; waste nothing.
6. **Industry** – Lose no time. Be always employed in something useful.
7. **Sincerity** – Use no hurtful deceit. Think innocently and justly.
8. **Justice** – Wrong none by doing injuries or omitting the benefits that are your duty.
9. **Moderation** – Avoid extremes.
10. **Cleanliness** – Tolerate no un-cleanliness in body, clothes, or habitation.

11. Tranquility – Be not disturbed by trifles or at accidents common or unavoidable.
12. Chastity – Rarely use venery [sex] but for health or offspring – never to dullness, weakness, or the injury of your own or another's peace or reputation.
13. Humility – Imitate Jesus and Socrates.

Another way to use this approach is to develop your own list. For example, one of the ways I use this concept is in running my business. Each week I pull, at random, out of my jar labeled "This Week's Focus," one of 13 activities written on a small piece of paper. Some of them are: Sell, Promote, Prospect, Write, and so on. Why not create your own list of attitudes or behaviors that you want to become a routine part of your life? It works.

Smart Thing #29

Learn from your mistakes.

> **Dumb Thing #30**
> **Seeing problems as negative.**

One of my heroes, the late Norman Vincent Peale, once said, "There is only one group of people that doesn't have problems and they are all dead. Problems are a sign of life. So, the more problems you have, the more alive you are." I would add, "If you don't have any problems, maybe you are on the way out of here and you don't know it yet."

This can be perceived as a tongue-in-cheek philosophy of life; however, it is closer to the truth than you might think. One thing you and I have both learned is that everyone has problems. Some people have relationship problems, others have financial ones; some face career challenges, others struggle with health problems; some have social issues, while others face difficult business challenges. No one is immune to adversity in life.

The key to success, happiness, peace, and life balance is to accept the issues, negatives, problems, situations, challenges, struggles (whatever you call them) as a part of the life process of becoming, learning, and growing. Failures, whiners, or victims see problems as life picking on them. Winners in life, regardless of their position, status, age, or circumstances see problems and adversity as a catalyst to becoming better, stronger, wiser, and more aware of the reality of their life.

Problems are not positive or negative; they are neutral. They are events. It isn't what is happening in your life that matters; it is how you choose to see it and what you do with it. Whether you perceive it as negative or positive is entirely up to you and your life outlook.

Learn to see the negatives as loving teachers in your life, bringing you the opportunity to get a clearer vision of where you may need attitude adjustments, improved thinking, or better skills.

> **Smart Thing #30**
> **Learn from adversity.**

Dumb Thing #31

Living in the past or future.

Life is lived in the present, one moment at a time, not in the past or future. Our futures and memories are created in all of our NOW moments. Living in the present means staying focused on what is happening now, not what happened yesterday, or may happen tomorrow.

People who focus on past mistakes, errors in judgment, words that were said with innocence, omissions, and disappointment tend to bring a great deal of negative energy into the present.

People who focus on future expectations, desires, hopes, and "some day" dreams tend to miss the value, joy, and wonder of their present moments.

Everyone has "stuff"; neither you nor anyone else will ever be rid of it all. The key is to understand that you can't fix what happened yesterday, and you can't fix anything tomorrow. You fix everything NOW.

Your soul wants for you what is your ultimate highest good. Your ego wants to look good, control, and protect itself. The ego tends not to like vulnerability and/or realness. This sets you up for hurt, pain, and rejection.

Learn to stay focused in the now. What you can do now. What you can say now. How you are feeling now. What you believe now. What you want to happen now.

Smart Thing #31

Stay focused in the present.

Chapter Two – Prospecting Dumb Things

Selling is a process.

One of the biggest problems for many salespeople is not understanding that selling is a process, not an event. Effective selling is not just closing the sale, better prospecting, or more effective sales presentations.

Although all of these are important in their own way, effective selling today means blending each of these together in such a way that the prospect trusts, believes, respects you and your organization, and wants and/or needs your product or service to help them improve the quality of their life or business enterprise.

For many years traditional sales training focused on the "close of the sale" as the most important element. Then the 70's and 80's rolled around, and the hot topic was prospecting, qualifying, and getting to the key decision makers. Then it was the 90's, and consultative selling. What will the next decade bring? Who knows for sure? What we do know now is that to sell successfully is only half of the task. The balance is keeping the business. Organizations expend millions of dollars annually to attract and sell new business. Then they lose it for any number of reasons and have to replace it. So the saga continues.

Selling is about finding good potential prospects who can benefit from your products/services, persuading them to buy from you, and then maintaining positive, ongoing relationships with them that ensure repeat and referral business as well as positive references. Are you focusing on only one particular aspect of the sales process as you sell? Are you weak in any particular part?

Each element of the process is intricately related to each other. For example, let's take prospecting. If you have a poor prospect, it will be difficult to give them a solid sales presentation. It will be impossible to overcome their sales objections, and as for closing the sale – forget it.

How about the attitude issues in the sales process? Let's say you lack confidence in the quality of your products. That will affect your willingness to find new prospects. If you do find some, it will impact your ability to give a confident sales presentation, etc., etc., etc.

How about one more? Let's say you have a fear of rejection. That will impact your willingness to ask questions, qualify your prospects, and discuss sales presentation issues that may be perceived as less than ideal. And asking for the order? Well, not in this lifetime.

I am sure you see my point. If you are going to sell successfully, you can't improve just one aspect of the sales process. You can't make up for poor prospecting with tricky closes. You can't make up for poor product knowledge with fancy footwork.

Since the skill of prospecting is the skill that ultimately contributes to success or frustration and failure, it is where we will begin in taking a look at the dumb things salespeople do in this area.

Remember, you will never turn a poor prospect into a customer with a great product or service, good presentation, or tricky close. However, a well-qualified prospect will help you sell them. One of the weakest areas of poor salespeople is the skill of prospecting. Master this, and the rest of the sales process will take care of itself.

Face adversity promptly and without flinching, and you will reduce its impact.

Winston Churchill

Dumb Thing #32

Selling only by the numbers.

For years, sales managers and sales trainers have been saying that sales is a "numbers" game. I can recall my first sales manager telling me over 35 years ago, "If you will see enough people, you will make enough sales." First of all, what's enough sales? Second of all, how many is enough people? Thirdly, is this the best approach to take to prospect for new business? This is why I hate clichés and managers and sales trainers who quote them only because that is what they have heard for years.

Now to my discovery: If you see enough *qualified* people, you will make enough sales. It isn't just the number, folks; it is focusing on prospects who qualify for your product or service. Now with this concept I am not suggesting that you should see fewer prospects. I am only suggesting that to just focus on the numbers alone will guarantee failure sooner or later. Why? The more people you see, the more you will tend to see who are poor prospects; thus, more rejection. The average salesperson can't handle the amount of rejection that comes with this philosophy. This is why so many people become discouraged and fail or quit.

Think about it for yourself for just a minute. You see/call 25 prospects a week. You close 1/5. That means you spent – whatever – amount of wasted time on 20 poor prospects. I know, I know: How do you know if they are poor prospects until you see or spend time with them? What if you took the time you spent with the 20 poor prospects and spent it with more good prospects – or even cultivating the five sales you made for repeat/referral business? See where I am going with this? Maybe your closing ratio could be 1/3 or even 1/2. Here is a real winner for success. Do both. See/call more prospects and make sure they are qualified before you give them too much of your time and energy.

Smart Thing #32

Prospecting is not how many people you see, but how good a prospect they are.

> **Dumb Thing #33**
> **Selling at the wrong level.**

A common mistake salespeople make is failing to recognize at what level they should be selling. There are five possible levels where you can direct your energy and time in the sales process:

1. The product/service level. This is where the salesperson focuses primarily on the price or features of the product or service and defines the product as a commodity. The typical reaction in this phase is to lower price due to a prospect's price resistance or competitive pressure.

2. The transaction level. This is where the salesperson sees the sales process in traditional terms: prospecting, presentation, overcoming objections, and closing the sale. In most cases, this approach still tends to focus on the process rather than the customer.

3. The solution level. This is where the salesperson brings a solution to the prospect/customer for their specific problem/need. Although this is better than selling at the transaction level, it still focuses on the relationship between the customer's needs and the features/benefits of the product/service.

4. The relationship level. Now we are getting more long-term-customer focused. Selling at this level requires patience, research, knowledge of the customer's short- and long-term agendas, time, effort, and a willingness to walk away from those sales where there is not a clear win/win/win outcome.

5. The stakeholder or shared fate level. Very few salespeople sell at this level. This is where, if your customer loses in any way, either directly or indirectly related to your product or service, you lose, also.

> **Smart Thing #33**
> **See effective selling not as a transaction,**
> **but as building relationships.**

Dumb Thing #34
Being a victim to sales cycles.

Many products and services have different sales cycles, from the first prospect meeting to the close of the sale. Some cycles can be several months to a few years. Some can be just a few days or a few hours.

Many salespeople believe that they are not in control of the sales cycle. They put the buying control into the hands of the prospect. Keep in mind that people buy when they are ready to buy, not when you need to sell.

First of all, remember that you do not change the prospect's buying needs, timetable, readiness, or urgency. You discover them. If your prospect has just signed a three-year contract with a competitor, guess what? This is not a prospect for you until the time when he begins to consider renewing or changing suppliers.

Most sales cycles are not etched in stone. They are a function of your ability to get to the real issues, needs, pain, and/or problems of your prospect. If you fail to identify these accurately, you will most likely never create the sense of urgency necessary to close sales sooner rather than later.

Don't get yourself into a mental rut that your sales cycle always has to be eight weeks, or six months, or seven days, or whatever. Those of you who believe that your normal buying cycle is, let's say, six months – I'll bet that you have closed sales in less time than that as well as more. The point is that the cycle is not a pre-determined period of time. It is a function of your ability to identify critical prospect issues and then show the prospect how you can satisfy in a way that can be accepted.

Smart Thing #34
Create a sense of buying urgency
to control sales cycles.

Dumb Thing #35

Thinking people buy from people they like.

Has selling really changed all that much in the past 50 years? Those of you who have been selling for less than five years most likely will answer that question with a NO. Those of you with battle scars going back into the 60's, 70's, and even the 80's, may answer with a resounding YES. Then there may be those of you who just are not sure or can't articulate it.

Some things have changed. Some have not. What has changed, from my perspective of over 35 years selling and teaching sales? Here are a few:

1. People have better, quicker, and easier access to information about your products/services and those of your competitors.
2. People want you to help them make better-informed decisions.
3. There are now three major segments of prospects: millions of baby boomers, millions of retired folks, and millions of people under the age of 35 who have lots and lots of money.
4. There are fewer layers of management to go through to get to your decision maker.
5. Technology is changing buyer buying patterns and attitudes.
6. People will not tolerate poor quality or poor service. They will do business with your competitor.
7. Your prospects have an increasing number of options, choices, and vendors from whom to purchase.

How about what hasn't changed?

People buy from people they trust.

Stop trying to get people to like you. Get them to trust you.

Smart Thing #35

Focus on establishing and building trust,
not on being liked.

> ### Dumb Thing #36
> ### Ignoring past clients.

Lost business does not necessarily mean lost forever. Many salespeople neglect this lucrative source of new business. I say *new* because, if you treat these past customers as new prospects, you may just regain their business. There are a number of reasons why customers leave you. Some of them are:

1. They were wooed away by a competitor offering better prices, service, or some promise.
2. Your organization has changed, and new management is not aware of the strengths of your services or products. This information was most likely not passed on to them by their predecessor.
3. You or your organization failed to deliver as promised.
4. You or your organization let trust and/or respect erode in the relationship.
5. There is some hidden agenda reason such as: They have a relative in the business, have lost buying authority, are leaving their organization for another position, etc.

There are others, but these are some of the ones you can control.

What can you do to regain this business?

1. First you must learn the REAL reason why the customer left.
2. You have to be willing to begin again.
3. You need to work as hard to *keep* the business as you did to *get* it.
4. You must re-assess where you went wrong. Was it a pricing issue, a service issue, a quality issue, a distribution issue, arrogance, ignorance, lack of interest in keeping the business, or some other major or minor mistake?
5. You must keep in touch with previous customers.

> ### Smart Thing #36
> ### Stay in touch with previous customers.

Dumb Thing #37

Staying in your comfort zone.

Over time, it can become easy to get stuck in one of a number of comfort zones when it comes to behavior, performance, techniques, or attitudes. Let's look at a few of the common ones to which many salespeople fall prey.

1. Calling only on clients or customers whom you like or who like you.
2. Selling only the products or services you make the most money on, know the most about, or are the easiest to sell.
3. Slowing down your sales activities at certain times of the month or year.
4. Adjusting your performance once you have exceeded your quota or your manager's expectations.
5. Avoiding new applications of your products or services.
6. Spending too much time with customers with whom you have a lot in common – despite their purchasing potential.
7. Having non-productive routines that keep you away from the real role of selling.
8. Spending too much time in after-sales service issues that keep you from selling more to new prospects.

List some of the areas in which you feel you are being locked in a comfort zone. After you have completed your personal list, answer the following:

1. How long have you had this behavior/attitude?
2. How is it sabotaging your sales success?
3. If continued, how will it impact your career (long term – short term)?
4. What can you do to change it?

Smart Thing #37

Be willing to try new and creative approaches to prospecting.

Dumb Thing #38
Letting lost business go without a fight.

We all lose business – from sales that are not closed, customers who decide to use a new supplier, businesses that no longer need our products or services, or for any number of other valid reasons. You cannot sell everyone and you cannot keep customers for life. To do so is a myth, no matter what you may have heard or read. The key is to not lose them because of poor performance, poor quality, poor service, or poor sales skills.

Some salespeople who lose a sale or a customer go into various irrational emotional reactions: They blame someone or everyone, make excuses, sulk, get angry, or run and hide. Successful salespeople understand the ebb and flow of business and relationships. If you have good sales skills, a good product or service, a positive attitude, a good prospect – sooner or later you will sell them.

Here are a few suggestions to use when you lose a sale:

1. Follow-up with a thank you note or letter.
2. Follow up with an after-sales critique or evaluation.
3. Follow up with additional proof sources, i.e. testimonials, articles, etc.
4. Find out what your competitor did better than you to get the business.
5. Don't assume/believe it was price, if that is what they tell you.
6. Don't let it negatively affect your attitude. Keep at it.

This week's lost business can be next month's sale. This month's lost customer can become next year's home run. You will win some and you will lose some. You won't win them all, and you won't lose them all. Just remember: Staying power over the long haul is much more beneficial than short-term quick success.

Smart Thing #38
Have a specific strategy for dealing with lost business.

> ## Dumb Thing #39
> ## Not routinely networking.

There is an old cliché that says, "It isn't *what* you know, but *who* you know that counts in the development of your career or business." I would like to change this to: It isn't who you know, but *who knows about you or your organization.*

You can know a lot of people, but if they don't know a great deal about you, the value of these contacts is limited. One of the keys to effective networking is the ability to both accumulate a variety of contacts in your data base and have these people aware of your skills, abilities, interests, and/or needs.

I have met tens of thousands of people in my 30-year career, but I would venture a guess that fewer than 500 can contribute to my success in some way by being able to introduce me to others they know who might be potential clients for me.

Networking is finding people who may be able to be a center of influence for you, taking the opportunity to get to know them, and giving them the opportunity to get to know you. Most salespeople are really poor networkers. They fail to join organizations where people congregate who could benefit them. Or, if they do belong, they fail to get involved or even participate in various meetings and networking opportunities.

How are you as a networker? Do you promote yourself with regularity in areas where influential people mingle? Do you belong to industry associations? Do you attend some of their meetings? Do you keep a database of contacts – where you met them and how they might be of value to you? Do you have some method to keep in touch with them (like a newsletter, periodic notes, telephone calls, use of email)?

> ## Smart Thing #39
> ## Develop a regular routine for finding and meeting new people who can help you.

Dumb Thing #40

Asking, "Did you get the information I sent?"

Customers and prospects have a great deal on their plates today. They have the demands of customers, bosses, fellow staff members, suppliers, and a variety of organizational, department, and industry issues that take a great deal of time and energy. When salespeople call on these busy prospects or clients, they must realize that what they are selling is not the most important thing in that prospect's life. Although the product/service might be of interest and value to them, salespeople must also do their essential follow-up. Why don't salespeople follow-up? Or when they do, why do they say dumb things like, "Did you get the literature I sent?" Da! Here's why:

1. They fear a "no" or a rejection.
2. They know the prospect is not going to buy.
3. They believe the prospect is too busy to talk with or see them.
4. They believe their competitors are going to get the business anyway.
5. They don't have an effective follow-up strategy.
6. They have nothing else to say.
7. They knew they had a poor prospect anyway, so why bother?

Guilty of any of these? It is easy to fall into the no-follow-up trap. Here are a few ideas to consider when you next follow up a sales call:

1. Don't begin with a closed-ended question like, "Have you made a decision yet?" Rather, "Where are you in the decision process?"
2. Don't ask, "Did you get the information that I sent?" Rather, "What is your impression of the information that I sent?"
3. Don't ask, "When can we get together to discuss our next step?" Rather, "Let's get together next Monday to…."
4. Don't ask, "Do you have any question about the proposal?" Rather, "Is there anything in the proposal that would prevent us from getting this order started?"

Smart Thing #40

Develop an effective follow-up strategy and use it.

Dumb Thing #41

Being afraid of rejection.

What is the number one cause of failure in sales? The inability to overcome the fear of rejection. Why do people let this fear negatively influence their behavior? Here are a few thoughts to consider:

1. Not everyone you try to sell to will want to buy from you.
2. Expecting everyone you meet to like or accept you is to live in fantasyland.
3. If you don't ask for anything – something – it is unlikely you will ever get it.
4. Does fear of rejection prevent you from asking probing questions, asking for an appointment, asking for the order?
5. The fear of rejection is an attitude issue and can be overcome only by strengthening other attitudes – such as confidence, self-belief, patience, trust, and self-image.
6. The fear of rejection is symptomatic of a need for acceptance.

Does the fear of rejection ever prevent you from:

1. Picking up the phone and making that next call?
2. Asking for the business?
3. Asking difficult probing questions?
4. Asking for referrals?
5. Asking for a bigger order?
6. Asking for a letter of testimony?
7. Asking for more responsibility in your position or a raise?
8. Following up on a customer who has had a problem?
9. Asking for an appointment with an important person?
10. Asking for a deposit?
11. Asking for a long-term contract?

Smart Thing #41

If you don't ASK, you may never receive.

Dumb Thing #42
Practicing on good prospects.

How much time do you spend practicing and developing your skills? Do you practice a new technique on a prospect or on a fellow salesperson or your supervisor first? Do you not practice at all or just show up? Show me any athlete in any sport who achieves success, fame, or even makes a decent living, and I will show you someone who spends more time practicing than in the performance of their sport. Here are a few examples.

Most Olympic athletes spend in excess of 3000 hours preparing for a 2-, 3-, or 10-minute race. Most good golfers hit hundreds of golf balls every day to refine their swing, balance, and performance. Baseball, basketball, or football teams practice for several hours 3-5 days a week, every week, for one 2-3-hour game. Are other careers different? No. Doctors, contractors, teachers, counselors, etc., spend time in research, discovery, and experimentation. They don't wait until they get into the operating room or in front of the classroom. Yours truly spends a minimum of 2-3 hours preparation for every hour in front of an audience.

Show me someone in any discipline who just shows up, and I will show you someone who is average at best, never makes a difference, and seldom achieves greatness. How about salespeople? What can they practice before a sales call? A telephone call? Much more:

1. New questions to ask prospects
2. New ways to ask those questions
3. How to cover the benefits of a product/service feature
4. How to create a sense of urgency
5. How to professionally terminate a presentation on a poor prospect
6. How to increase a sale by "up-selling"
7. How to better answer a prospect's questions

Smart Thing #42
Practice new techniques on a fellow salesperson.

> **Dumb Thing #43**
> **Talking too much.**

One of the biggest mistakes poor salespeople make is THEY TALK TOO MUCH. The second is: THEY GIVE INFORMATION BEFORE THEY GET IT. When you make these mistakes, you will tend to turn off most potential customers or clients.

A product- or organizational-driven sales approach is when your focus is on giving information rather than getting it. A customer-driven presentation is when you get more information than you give, and the information you give is what the prospect needs or wants to hear, not what you want to tell them.

The key to your success is not in the delivery of a pre-planned message that covers all the features that some genius in your organization has decided are important. The key to your success is to discover what your prospect's needs, issues, concerns, problems, wants, desires, or attitudes are. Then deliver only that information that they need in order to make an intelligent buying decision now. Give them the rest of the stuff later – if they want it.

When you talk too much, you will give unnecessary or wrong information. Learn to let the prospect drive the process; not the control of it, but the information portion.

Another myth or way of stating this is the outdated sales axiom: Plan your sales calls.

Don't plan the information you are going to give. If you have been selling your product or service for a year or more, you shouldn't need to plan. However, plan the information you need to get and the questions you are going to ask.

> **Smart Thing #43**
> **The prospect should be talking**
> **at least twice as much as you are.**

Dumb Thing #44

Losing control of the sales process.

There are many ways salespeople lose control of the sales process. Here are a few for your consideration:

1. They quote price – just because the prospect has asked (before they have had a chance to build value).
2. They don't ask enough questions early in the sales process. They just ramble on.
3. They send out literature when asked, without first qualifying the prospect.
4. They don't get deposits and they hope the prospect will pay someday.
5. They leave "will calls" (call me back) when telephoning a prospect.

Control is one of the key elements for success in sales. Successful salespeople understand that control is not manipulation, but is in the ultimate best interests of the prospect or client. I will bet you have a prospect right now, as you are reading this, with whom you have lost control. You are waiting for this prospect to respond to your offer, appeal, or whatever. How do you get and keep control? The best time to get control of the sales process with a new prospect is in the early stages of the relationship. It is very difficult to get it back later. One of the best strategies is to resist the tendency to jump from information getting to information giving in the presentation.

Successful salespeople determine not only the buying habits and payment philosophy of the prospects and clients they have, but also the respect they receive and the manner in which they are treated by these prospects/clients. Some of you may have some clients you wish you didn't have. Right? Pay attention to early signals and remember that you and I have what our prospects want and need: solutions to their needs and problems. So keep control of the buying process.

Smart Thing #44

Keep control with a planned approach.

Dumb Thing #45

Acting like you need the business.

Sounding pathetic is one of the surest ways to ensure that your customer will lack confidence and respect for both you and your organization. People buy when they are ready to buy, not when you need to sell. It is essential that in every sales situation that you always put the prospect or customer ahead of your needs.

Begging is not attractive.

You beg when you say things like:

- "What time is convenient for you?" Rather, "Let's see if we can arrange a mutually beneficial time."

- "We're the best in the business." Rather, "Let's see how our product or service will solve your problem."

- "When can you let me know your decision?" Rather, "Let's set a time to discuss your decision."

- "Can I call you in a few weeks to follow-up?" Rather, "I'll call you in a few weeks to discuss your questions and further interest."

- "We can't do that. It's against company policy." Rather, "Let's see how we can accomplish this."

There are thousands of ways to sound insecure and unprofessional. All of them send the message that you lack confidence in your ability to perform and your credibility.

Smart Thing #45

Keep the focus on how the customer benefits.

Dumb Thing #46
Not building trust early.

As I asked earlier: Has selling really changed all that much in the past 50 years? Those of you who have been selling for less than five years most likely will answer that question with a NO. Those of you with battle scars going back into the 60's, 70's and even the 80's, may answer with a resounding YES. Then there may be those of you who just are not sure or can't articulate it.

Some things have changed. Some have not. What has changed, from my perspective of over 35 years selling and teaching sales? Here are a few:

1. People have better, quicker and easier access to information about your products/services and those of your competitors.
2. People want you to help them make better informed decisions.
3. More women are in positions of influence.
4. There are increased opportunities to sell to people from different cultures.
5. There are fewer layers of management to go through to get to your decision maker.
6. Technology is changing buyer buying patterns and attitudes.
7. Your prospects have an increasing number of options, choices and vendors from whom to purchase.

How about what hasn't changed?

1. People still buy what they want and desire.
2. People still want a fair value.
3. People do not want to be lied to or misled.
4. People do not want to pay too much to solve their problem or satisfy their wants/needs.
5. PEOPLE BUY FROM PEOPLE THEY TRUST.

Smart Thing #46
Establish the prospect's trust before you begin to sell.

Dumb Thing #47

Not asking elevator questions.

What are elevator questions? Let me answer by asking you a question: If you were told by a prospect that you had 60 seconds to sell them, what would you do? Would you condense your sales message into a one-minute presentation or talk about your organization and its strengths and history? Would you ask a few thought-provoking questions or sit or stand there dumbfounded, wondering what to do or what to say next?

I recently met a prospect on an elevator in a Las Vegas hotel at a speaking engagement. He looked like he was a business-type person so I asked him, "What do you do for a living?" He responded, "I am in the insurance industry." My follow-up question was, "What do you do in the insurance business" He said he was the president. (Keep in mind, I don't have a lot of time here; we are on an elevator.)

My follow-up question was, "Do you know what your lost sales are costing you every year" (This is an Elevator Question.)

He responded with a pause, then answered, "I am not sure. What do you do for a living?"

I said, "I am in the business of helping organizations reduce their lost sales revenue" (Elevator Statement). An elevator question is any question that cuts to the heart of your prospect's challenges, concerns, or fears and makes them think. It also implies that you or your organization may have a possible solution for their problems. Remember that elevator questions are not used only on elevators. They can be used at social settings, while selling on the telephone, or anywhere during the sales process. All of the great salespeople I have ever met or had the privilege of having in my audiences were masters at elevator questions.

Smart Thing #47

Develop several urgency-building, probing elevator questions.

Dumb Thing #48
Not getting to the decision maker.

One of the biggest time wasters in sales is when salespeople fail to get to the real decision-makers and present their products and/or services to people who cannot say *yes* or can only say *no.* Since many organizations are undergoing sweeping changes in management and in the way they purchase from vendors, it is increasingly difficult to identify who is really in charge. I am not suggesting that, at certain times in the sales process, it is inappropriate to give a presentation to someone who can only recommend your products. I do suggest you keep in mind that every time you present to a non-decision maker, you lose an important ingredient in the sales process: CONTROL.

Back to decision makers. There are two prospecting strategies you can follow. Bottom-up or top-down prospecting. In bottom-up you start anywhere in the organization where someone will see you. In top-down, you begin with the senior person and work down. I have found that, once you have identified a prospect as qualified, the best approach is both top-down and bottom-up simultaneously. The bottom-up portion is the easier of the two. It is here where you gather additional pertinent information about needs, wants, current suppliers, etc. Top-down is where you sell the big picture.

When I call a new prospect, I ask the contact, "Who is the person in your organization making the buying decision about *x*?" My next question is, "Who is that person's supervisor?" The next step is easy. I say thank you and call back and ask for the supervisor. It could be the President, Senior VP, or CEO; it doesn't matter. I am looking for the ultimate decision-maker at that location: i.e. branch, division, subsidiary – whatever. Without getting to the ultimate economic buyer, you are only logging sales calls that may never go anywhere.

Smart Thing #48
Give presentations only to those
who make buying decisions.

Dumb Thing #49

Not knowing your competitors.

Many salespeople tend to see their competition as only those businesses selling a similar product, service, or idea. In other words, salespeople selling computers tend to see their competitors as other computer stores, retailers, or manufacturers. People selling insurance, travel, furniture – you name it – whatever you sell, you need to know that your competition is not just your direct competitors, but anyone and everyone who is trying to get a piece of the corporate or consumer dollar.

I can recall years ago, when I was just beginning my career as a speaker and trainer, I lost my first big sales training contract to a salesperson selling *computer hardware*. In my sales approach, I strategically positioned my features and benefits so that any other speaker/trainer would have difficulty successfully competing with me. Problem was, I was successful at keeping my fellow speakers and trainers at bay, but ultimately lost the sale to someone who was selling something totally unrelated to training. I asked myself, where did I go wrong?

It was simple: I saw my competitors as people who sold only what I was selling. WRONG. My prospect, the company president, told me that the training program I was selling was important to him and they would keep it on the back burner for the short term. Upgrading all of their computer hardware was more important to him now. What's the answer? If you are going to continue to succeed and prosper in sales, you have to be better, smarter, quicker, more flexible, more resilient, etc., etc., than every salesperson in your territory, no matter what they sell. Just being better than the people selling copiers, if you sell copiers, is not enough.

Smart Thing #49

Learn everything about all of your competitors.

Dumb Thing #50

Failing to build psychological debt.

One of my early lessons in sales happened over 40 years ago. I was getting lots of feedback like, "Tim, you are really good at this." "You are going to be really successful in this business." "You really know your stuff." Kind words, yes. Sales, NO. I went to a good friend who was making over a million dollars a year selling insurance and told him of my plight: lots of compliments, no orders. This is, as best as I can recall, his advice:

"Tim, when you give a sales presentation to a prospect, are you nice to them? Do you give them your time? Do you educate them? Do you give them the benefit of your experience?" Etc., etc. My answers to all of his questions were, "Yes." "Here is what is happening. You are building a psychological debt. They owe you, and the way they pay off the debt is with a compliment. Once you accept the compliment, the debt is paid." Thus, no order. Well, I couldn't feed my kids compliments, so I said, "Larry, what do I do?" His response, "Refuse their compliments. You see, when you do not accept the compliments, the debt still exists." "How do I do that, Larry?"

"Say to your prospect something to the effect, 'If I were that good, we would be doing business together." Or, "If I am going to be that successful, I would be better able to communicate the benefits of my proposal to you. I am sorry, but I don't deserve that compliment." He continued, "Now, when you get a compliment *and* an order, say 'Thank you very much.'" This one piece of advice helped more in my sales career than dozens of the books I had read and seminars I had attended. Don't let your prospect off the psychological hook that easily. What you want and need is business, not validation, approval, acceptance, or appreciation.

Smart Thing #50

Create psychological debt through service.

Dumb Thing #51

Lacking a precise call-back approach.

Earlier I introduced the subject of failing to do the essential follow-up (see Dumb Thing #41). More often than I can state, over the years when I have followed up with a prospect who has been considering my services, I have heard, "Thanks for getting back to me. I had every intention of calling you, but have just been too busy. Let's get this program rolling." Why don't salespeople follow-up? And what are the benefits of an effective follow-up strategy? These are two critical issues that will determine the success of salespeople. What are some more reasons salespeople don't follow up?

1. They are too disorganized and are not even aware that they should follow up.
2. They lack confidence in themselves or their organization and its services or products.
3. They believe their competitors are going to get the business anyway.

If you are guilty of any of these, here are a few ideas to consider when you next follow up a sales call:

1. Don't open with a closed ended question like, "Have you made a decision yet?" Rather, "Where are you in the decision process?"
2. Don't ask, "Did you get the information that I sent?" Rather, "What is your impression of the information that I sent?"
3. Don't ask, "When can we get together to discuss our next step?" Rather, "Let's get together next Monday to….."

What, then, are the benefits of an effective follow-up strategy?

1. Increased sales.
2. You look more professional.
3. You beat the competition.

Smart Thing #51

Have an effective follow-up strategy.

Dumb Thing #52
Not asking for referrals.

It is easier, less stressful, less costly, and less time consuming to sell to qualified referrals than to any other source of prospects. It is amazing how many salespeople fail to make asking for referrals a regular part of their selling behavior. Getting referrals is not rocket science. Although there are several methods to generate referral business, the best way I know of is to just ask.

I have surveyed my sales audiences for over 25 years by asking them, "How many would like to have more referrals?" I always get a unanimous show of hands. My next question is, "Why don't you have them?" and the answer is always, "I don't ask." Referrals can come from anywhere: customers, non-competing salespeople or suppliers, friends, relatives, your banker, neighbor, and even Aunt Sally.

There is no wrong time to ask for referrals. Many salespeople feel that to ask for referrals from customers, they must have first provided the service or product in a satisfactory way. Why wait to ask? Every minute you are not creating a referral-awareness in the minds of your customers or other sources, your competitors might be one step ahead of you.

Timing is important in selling. Every minute you lose discovering a new prospect that will benefit from your produce or service brings you closer to missing out on additional business.

Don't wait. There are several ways to generate referrals. You can call a customer, write them, email them, fax them, or visit them for the sole purpose of asking for referrals. Why not set some specific goals to generate a certain number of referrals every week for the next several weeks until the habit is a permanent part of your regular selling routine.

Smart Thing #52
Ask every customer and prospect for referrals.

Dumb Thing #53

Not using a prospect profile.

Prospecting has two basic elements: identification and qualification.

Identification is finding potential customers that have the need, desire, ability to pay for your products/services, the willingness to see you, and who can either make the buying decision or contribute significantly toward it. Qualification is: a) the strategies used to determine which of the prospects you have identified are the best prospects in whom to invest your time, energy, and resources now, and b) discovering the information needed to develop a sales strategy and approach that will enable you to tailor your presentation to the needs, desires, problems, concerns, and buying style of your prospect.

If you sell a product or service to the general consumer, the identification process can be a time consuming and difficult process. Of the thousands of people you could see, which ones – from a cursory first look – would make it past the qualification process?

If you sell to the business community, health care industry, the government, or any other major business segment – whether regionally, nationally, or globally – the identification process is as easy as perusing a directory or custom data base, or searching a specific mailing list for those prospects that meet your general criteria.

A system I have used successfully for over 30 years is to build an "ideal prospect profile." This is developed by evaluating the characteristics of your best customers and then creating a profile or template that you work towards while both identifying and qualifying each potential prospect for as close a match as possible to that profile.

Smart Thing #53

Use a systematic method for qualifying prospects.

Dumb Thing #54

Not becoming a resource.

In a highly competitive international business climate, it is essential that salespeople become even more creative in finding ways to service their clients. One principle to keep in mind is that it is easier, less stressful, less time consuming, and less expensive to do more business with a present client than it is to keep looking for new clients.

One of the best ways I have discovered to reduce client turnover and generate repeat business, referrals, and the right to use the client as a reference is to be a better resource for your client. A newsletter is one example of being a resource. Here's another: Recently I have sent three articles to other authors on a variety of topics that I thought would interest them. My cost: around $1.00 per mailing. The return: additional business, referrals, and references. Find ways to be a better resource for your customers and watch your business grow. Here are some examples to get you started:

1. Send articles that you think will interest your client.
2. Send books and audio tapes that will contribute to their knowledge.
3. Conduct training seminars for their employees.
4. Keep them abreast of industry trends, forecasts, and competitive information.
5. Bring them business.
6. Give them a subscription to a publication in an area that interests them.
7. Provide your home and mobile telephone numbers.
8. Be willing to go the extra mile. Promise a lot and deliver more.
9. Send special greeting cards for birthdays, business anniversaries, etc.
10. Share any information with your customers that will contribute to their success.

Smart Thing #54

Be a business resource for all of your customers.

Chapter Three – Sales Presentation Dumb Things

I recall that in my first sales position, we were trained by a national organization, a leader in its industry, to "memorize" the sales presentation and we were then instructed to go out and tell the company story (giving the presentation we had learned). That industry at the time had a 95% turnover ratio of new salespeople in the first year.

I was one of those in the 95% who was let go. No wonder. Don't sell anything for six months and you might begin to think you should have taken up another career. Well, I went back into the same business and within one year was an industry leader. How? Simple, I changed my focus from selling my company and its strengths and product features to determining what my prospect's needs, wants, and desires were.

But beware. Selling today has, in many cases, become like a giant shell game, or what I refer to as the Big Pow Wow. For those of you who haven't got a clue as to what I am talking about, let me explain. Years ago, when the white man invaded the Native Americans' homeland, they would often bring gifts. These gift exchanges were accomplished with various ritualistic behaviors on the part of both parties. When all was said and done, if the white man escaped with his head, it was a good day. *Both* parties were selling: the Native Americans, the right to trespass, hunt, or even live; and the white invaders, their goods and trinkets from the East.

Flash forward 200-250 years and what have we got? You and I are trading what we have (the product or service we provide, that our customer wants or needs) for their wampum (money).

Some Native Americans, without the benefit of attending the latest seminar on effective negotiation, were quite persuasive when it came to getting more of what they wanted. The white men often walked away, after giving a great deal, with the feeling that they had been taken to the cleaners. Today, many salespeople give away far too much – in the way of margins, discounts and extra services – to satisfy the demands or expectations of the prospect. They treat the sales process like a big shell game or old-fashioned Pow Wow.

Customers today want value, not trinkets; service, not empty words; honest commitments, not temporary involvement; and fair treatment, not selfish demands.

In an age where competition abounds, choices are increasing, and quality, service, and timely communication are the hallmarks of positive relationships, salespeople can no longer afford to live with the illusions that they can get by with giving World Series tickets, dinners at expensive restaurants, or special gifts. People are as smart now as they were 200 years ago, maybe even smarter.

Be careful not to fall into the trap of giving away more than is necessary. Most customers today would rather have a fair price, good value, and professional treatment far more than all of this other "stuff."

If you want to ride off into the sunset with your head where it belongs – on top of your shoulders – become familiar with what your customers really want, not what you think they want or may even tell you they want.

The first ingredient in communication is truth, the second, good sense, the third, good humor, and the fourth, wit.

Sir Wm. Temple

Dumb Thing #55

Not giving tailored presentations.

One of the biggest mistakes poor salespeople make is that they talk too much. They launch into a "feature dump" covering a litany of features. But a persuasive sales presentation is nothing more than a conversation with a specific agenda. It is a process of discovering what your prospects want, need, and are concerned about, and relating these to the particular aspects of your product or service.

If you have four sales appointments today, each presentation should be totally different. Oh, the structure might be similar, but the content or what you cover should be specific to the customer. A good sales presentation:

1. Is brief and focused
2. Comes from the prospect's perspective – not yours or the organization's
3. Is a two-way conversation and interactive
4. Blends the right amount of emotional appeal (customer benefits) with logical reasons to buy (features and product benefits)
5. Involves the prospect, allowing them to develop some ownership of or comfort with the product or service
6. Ties the customer benefits back to their Dominant Emotional Buying Motive
7. Tests the attitudes or acceptance of the prospect with assumptive phrases and trial closes
8. Approaches the prospect from their personality style comfort level
9. Is Tailored, Tailored, Tailored

An effective sales presentation is not an "unloading" of information on the prospect. Remember, if a prospect knows what you sell and will see you, he has bought. If he doesn't, it is because you missed something!

Smart Thing #55

Tailor each presentation to the client's specific desires.

Dumb Thing #56
Not having a concise defining statement.

A defining statement is a very specific and precise clarifying statement. It combines all of the necessary ingredients so that when a prospect walks away from an elevator conversation with you, he knows who you are, what you do, and how he will benefit by doing business with you.

A defining statement should include all of the following ingredients:

1. *It must use common one-syllable words that are easy to understand.*
   If you stick to the language an 8th grader would understand (and I am not referring here to slang), you are in good shape.

2. *It must be conversational.*
   It is not an advertising theme or slogan; it is a conversational answer to the question, "What do you do?"

3. *It must create some attraction on the part of the other person.*
   It should make people want to talk with you, be with you, learn from you.

4. *It must have a dream focus.*
   If it helps the prospect see the future as better than the present in any way, you have a dream focus.

5. *It must contain the* what *and the* who.
   It defines outcomes and who would be served by working with you or buying from you.

6. *It must have a dual focus.*
   Create a two-part statement that has two outcomes and you will thereby appeal to a wider audience.

Here is my own defining statement that illustrates all of the above points:

I own a business that's purpose is to help our clients increase their sales and improve their management focus and effectiveness.

Take your time developing your defining statement. This one took me several hours over a period of a few weeks. But, once you have it, now let it get a hold of you and believe it, memorize it, practice it, use it, and watch it galvanize the people with whom you interact.

Smart Thing #56
Know exactly what to say,
regardless of the circumstances.

Dumb Thing #57

Selling low price rather than high value.

Most poorly trained salespeople tend to lower the price when they receive price resistance. The price will always seem high to a prospect or customer if the perceived value is low. The key to effectively handling price resistance is to understand this simple, yet profound, concept.

People say they want low price, but what they really want is low cost. What is the difference?

Low price is what customers pay for your product or service now. Low cost is what they pay for it over time. For example, when they buy an inexpensive piece of equipment to save money, but it is in constant need of repair because it breaks down frequently. Although they may have saved money initially, their cost over time will be much higher than if they had invested more in a better piece of equipment.

In most cases, we get what we pay for. Buy cheap and you get less value or higher cost. Buy expensive and you get higher value or lower cost over time.

What are you selling, high value or low cost? Personally, I would rather sell a high-priced product or service than a low-priced one. It is much easier to justify high price if the value is there, than poor quality and constant product/service problems.

Remember, the key to success in selling is building strong relationships. Poor quality, even though customers save money initially, is not in their best long-term interests. How do you want to be remembered by your customers? For low quality – or for a good value at a fair price?

Smart Thing #57

Create high perceived value so price is not an issue.

Dumb Thing #58

Selling features and not customer benefits.

Product or service features are what the product or service is. Product benefits are what the features do for the product. Customer benefits are what the features and product benefits do for the customer.

Prospects need to know what the features are, but they buy because of what those features do for them; i.e., the customer benefits. Most salespeople sell features. A few of the better salespeople sell product benefits. The very successful salespeople sell customer benefits.

What's the difference? Here is a simple presentation of all three.

"Mr. Prospect, one of the exceptional features of our product is that it is made of steel." (Feature) "This gives the product durability." (Product benefit) "What this means to you is that it will last a long time and require very little maintenance." (Customer benefit)

Just giving the prospect a list of features may educate them on your service, but it won't get them to buy. Giving them the product benefits will help them understand the value of the service, but it won't get the sale closed. The key is to develop a presentation strategy that covers all three from the customer's point of view. There are two problems when it comes to a feature-based presentation:

1. Prospects will never picture themselves owning or using the service.
2. This approach makes it easier for them to use price as a reason not to buy.

I suggest you do two things regarding this part of the sales process:

1. Make a list of all of your features – yes, all of them.
2. Create a customer-focused benefit statement around each feature.

Smart Thing #58

Ensure the prospect understands what is in it for them.

Dumb Thing #59
Selling everyone the same.

A common mistake many salespeople make is that they sell to everyone in the same way. These salespeople fail to take into consideration that each buyer or prospect has very individual motives and/or reasons for buying what they do, when they do, and how they do. One of the keys to effective selling is to sell the prospect the way they are comfortable buying, not the way you are comfortable selling. Let me explain further.

There are four major types of buyers: 1) ones who want quick answers and the bottom line; 2) those who want lots of details and information and accuracy; 3) those who want to create a relationship with you and get to know you; and 4) those who want to make buying a social event and want to have fun.

Each of these four types of buyers must be approached from their perspective or comfort zone. To give a ton of information on features and benefits to a prospect who wants only the bottom line will surely put you back on the street with a NO SALE. To expect a fast decision – waltz in, give your presentation, and waltz out – with the relationship buyer will earn their contempt and lack of trust. The secret, and it really isn't a secret at all, is to have four – that's right, FOUR – distinct selling styles, vocabularies, approaches, and presentations.

Your prospect will tell you what you need to tell them to sell them, but you must discover their buying style before you launch into your presentation. Not only must you present differently to the four, you must also close them, service them, negotiate with them, and treat them uniquely. In one of my recent seminars, one of the participants came up to me during a break after we had discussed this idea and said, "I do all of this naturally." I hate to burst your illusion, but our tendency is to sell out of our own unique approach and not tailor our presentation to different buyer's styles.

Smart Thing #59
Customize your sales message and approach.

Dumb Thing #60
Not relating to the prospect.

If you have been in sales for more than six months, you have most likely heard from a manager or some other salesperson: "You have to start every presentation with some small talk. You have to break the ice, get to know them, or make them comfortable." Yes and no!

Some prospects want to get to know you and you them. Others just want their problems solved or needs and desires satisfied. Spending time in *Getting to know you* with prospects who do not want this is doomed to cause you to fail or at least lose valuable selling momentum.

The key is to know how your prospect wants you to relate to them. I recommend that you begin every presentation with a simple question, and I don't care whether you are selling Lear jets or Tupperware.

"Ms. Prospect, I don't know how I and my organization can best be of service to you; the only way for me to determine that is if I can ask you a few questions. Is that OK?"

This approach does two very important things in the sales process:

1. It gives you control. (The person who asks the questions controls the conversation. The person who talks the most dominates it. And in a sales situation you want to control it, not dominate it.)
2. It gets the prospect talking and keeps them talking.

In my career I have discovered that poor prospects don't want a lot of questions; they just want you to get to the price. Good prospects want you to know what their needs, problems, circumstances, or wants are and if you can satisfy them.

You'll never know, and they will never know, if you do all of the talking.

Smart Thing #60
Always come from the prospect's perspective.

> **Dumb Thing #61**
> **Seeing the sale as a transaction.**

Poor salespeople focus on just closing the sale. Successful salespeople focus on creating relationships. Which is your approach?

Selling is not only about closing the current prospect on a particular product or service that solves one of their pressing problems, needs, or desires. It is about building a trusting relationship and partnership with them by becoming a resource and helping them solve their on-going problems, or satisfying their continuing and evolving needs and desires.

You must first evaluate your selling intent or philosophy underlying the sales process, and how it impacts your ability to close this sale and the future relationship. If your focus is on the short term vs. the long term, your intent is most likely only on moving products or services now. If your intent is to develop a long-term, mutually beneficial relationship with this new prospect, you may not sell this order, but that does not prevent you from beginning to build a positive relationship that can one day end in success.

It takes more time, resources, and energy to generate a new customer than it does in keeping an existing one. It is also easier to do more business with a present customer than it is to find more new ones. What is your approach? Are you investing a greater proportion of your time and resources to continue to find new business, or to satisfy, develop, and keep existing business? I agree that a continual flow of new business is the lifeblood of growth and success in sales; however, don't underestimate the ability to use your present customers to help you with that mission. Next, few customers will just give you their business. You must ask for it, but you also have to earn the right to get it. In my opinion, closing is more of a philosophy than a skill. It is more an attitude than a strategy. It is more about giving than getting, and it is more about service than your sales compensation.

> **Smart Thing #61**
> **See the sale as part of an ongoing relationship.**

> ### Dumb Thing #62
> ### Invalidating prospects.

What is an invalidator? It is a person who puts other people down, insults them even subtly, disregards their opinions, does not listen, let's their own ego try to control the other person, is emotionally manipulative, or negates their feelings. How do you know if you if you tend to invalidate people?

1. Do you interrupt prospects while they are talking?
2. Are you an active listener regardless of who is speaking or how?
3. Is your ego – the need to be right, look good – getting in your way?
4. Are you more concerned with your need to make the sale than with the prospect's needs?

What are the consequences of being an invalidator in sales? Let me give you a couple of illustrations that I witnessed in actual live sales presentations:

1. At the end of a product presentation to UPS, the salesperson said, "Tell you what, I'll FedEx a sample to you so you have it tomorrow to review." Dumb? Yes. Invalidation? Yes. How? Well, he sent the subtle signal that FedEx was more reliable than UPS to ship the sample. Now whether he believed that really doesn't matter. He lost the sale.
2. While making a presentation to a Pepsi-cola distributor, the prospect asked the salesperson if she would like something to drink. Before she realized what she had said, she blurted out, "Sure, Id love a Coke." Dumb? Yes. Invalidation? Yes. For the same sort of reason as above.

There are hundreds of ways salespeople invalidate prospects every day. Ever say, "Let me repeat"? This assumes the prospect is deaf or stupid.

> ### Smart Thing #62
> ### Treat prospects with respect and concern.

> **Dumb Thing #63**
> **Not listening.**

Hearing and listening are two different things. Hearing is a physical act. Listening is a mental one. The ears collect sound waves and send them to the brain for interpretation. If you don't have a hearing problem, it doesn't necessarily mean you are a good listener.

One of the biggest complaints many prospects have about salespeople is that they don't listen. Why don't people listen?

1. They don't care about the other person.
2. They are more concerned with their own ideas or thoughts.
3. It takes too much work to listen, so they just fake it.
5. They don't know how to listen.
6. They think they are listening.
8. Their ego (the need to manipulate, control, or look good) gets in the way of their listening.
9. The other person's non-verbal communication style gets in the way.
10. They think they know more about the subject than the person who is talking.
11. They are preoccupied with their own stuff.

One of the greatest compliments you can pay a prospect or customer is to be willing to listen to them regardless of their speaking style, pace, education, or emotional circumstances.

Are you a good listener? One way to find out is to ask others to comment on your listening willingness and ability.

> **Smart Thing #63**
> **Hang on the prospect's every word**
> **to ensure understanding.**

> **Dumb Thing #64**
>
> **Having a poor vocabulary.**

The tools of the professional salesperson are words. We paint word pictures, we tell stories, we describe product or service features and benefits, we influence, we inspire, and we hope to convince people of the benefits of doing business with us. All of this requires a command of language. It amazes me how many salespeople have poor vocabularies. These people fail to realize that they are limiting their success, negatively impacting their destiny and life style by not having the ability to use the right word at the right time in any communication situation.

The key is to have a good enough vocabulary to be able to effectively communicate with people who have either an outstanding vocabulary or a poor one. In both cases, we need to be able to use effective words that can be understood by our prospect or customer. The ability to articulate your feelings, attitudes, needs, skills, desires, and knowledge is one of the most important ingredients for success in sales and in life.

How is your vocabulary? Do you often find you overuse certain words because you lack the ability to use replacement words? Do you ever find yourself searching for just the right word for a particular situation? Is your vocabulary getting in the way of your future success? Do you tend to use, or overuse, profanity?

Here are a few ways to enlarge your vocabulary: crossword puzzles, Scrabble, reading magazines, learning one new word a day (that's 365 new words a year). In five years, imagine what kind of a vocabulary you could have with that technique. When someone uses a word you are unfamiliar with, ask what it means. Get a daily calendar that gives you a new word a day. There are also audio albums on vocabulary improvement.

> **Smart Thing #64**
>
> **Know the power of words**
>
> **and how they contribute to success.**

Dumb Thing #65
Failing to create a sense of urgency.

One of the critical factors in a successful sales outcome is the sense of urgency a prospect brings to the sales process. A question I have been asked many times in my sales seminars is: Can you create a sense of urgency? Yes, but it takes skill and effective communication ability, right attitudes, product knowledge, and confidence.

What is a sense of urgency? You discover, for example, that your prospect's primary supplier is back-ordered and they need the supplies yesterday.

Urgency means the prospect needs a solution, answer, product, service NOW. Price is not the main issue, terms are not the issue. Your ability to deliver according to their needs or expectations is the ONLY issue. Why do many salespeople spend literally hours every week in front of prospects that have no sense of urgency? Yes, you have to spend some time with them to determine if there is a sense of urgency, but once you discover there isn't, or you can't create it – NEXT. (That's: Move on to the next prospect, the sooner the better.)

How can you create a sense of urgency? By focusing on the critical business factors, weaknesses, problems and needs, and showing the prospect how waiting will cost them more than they are going to want to pay if they wait. Let's look back at one of the above examples. Let's assume that the current supplier is not back-ordered with the products your prospect needs. Here are a couple of questions to ask your prospect:

1. What would happen if your current supplier couldn't deliver?
2. Do you have a secondary source of supply should your current supplier let you down?

Smart Thing #65
Learn the prospect's dominant emotional buying motive.

Chapter Four –
Handling Objections & Closing Dumb Things

Have you ever computed the cost of your lost sales revenue in a week or year?

My 30-year research of the ratio of my clients' sales efforts to sales income – regardless of industry, organization size, individual sales experience, and market conditions – shows that the average salesperson has a 1-to-5 closing ratio on new prospects. If you are doing better than that, congratulations! If not, please read on.

Tens of thousands of ineffective sales calls are made every day by well-meaning but poorly-trained salespeople. One of the common reasons why salespeople do not close more sales is the inability to effectively disarm sales resistance in advance or overcome sales objections during the sales process.

The extrapolated cost of lost revenue in a year from these lost sales is staggering, to say the least. I have developed a simple formula that helps you determine how much actual revenue you are losing or how much your sales group is losing in a year. I recommend you compute this number only if you are a hardy soul and on some kind of high-blood-pressure medicine.

1. Subtract the number of closed sales from the total number of presentations given to good prospects in a week by you or one of your average salespeople.
2. Now multiply the remaining number (lost sales) by your average sales income per closed customer. Granted, this number will vary, but it will give you a good indicator. If you don't know the average income per customer, determine that first. This will give you the lost total revenue for yourself or an average sales rep in a week.
3. If you are a sales manager or executive: Now multiply that number times the total number of sales reps in your sales force. This will give you the total of lost revenue for the week by your combined sales group.
4. Now multiply this number times 52 and bingo, you've got the magic number of your lost revenue or the lost revenue of your sales team in a year.

Here is an example for a typical rep:

- 12 appointments per week, 3 sales, 9 no sales
- Average income per sale: $1000
- Lost revenue by this rep in one week: $9,000
- As a manager, if you have 10 reps, that's $90,000 in lost revenue in one week.
- Times 52 weeks: that's $4,680,000 in lost revenue in one year.

We only used $1000 for an average sale. You can imagine what the number would be if your average sale was much higher!

I understand that:

- Every product/service has a different sales cycle.
- Every product/service has more or less competition.
- Every organization has more or less corporate resources required for support and sales costs.
- Every sales rep has a unique territory.
- Every sales rep has a different level of competence.

But, the point remains: Even if you used better than average numbers and favorable sales conditions, I guarantee your revenues per week and year or the revenues of your salespeople could be much – much – higher.

Learning to effectively handle sales resistance is one of the best ways to improve your sales results. Naturally, it is important to be trying to close a good prospect rather than a poor one, but we have covered the prospecting and qualification issue in a previous chapter.

Keep in mind that the frequency, number, and type of sales objections are excellent clues that will help you determine whether you have a good prospect or a bad one.

Dumb Thing #66

Not disarming objections early.

There are only two ways to handle sales resistance: Answer objections when they come up or disarm them in advance. Which do you think is the most effective approach? Traditional sales training for many years has suggested that salespeople should develop a number of pat answers to common sales objections and then, when these objections surface, give your memorized response. Although this strategy may be effective from time to time, there is a much better method for handling these potential sales busters.

In order to disarm sales objections, you need to know what they are *before* they become your prospect's focal point. A dumb approach is to give your presentation to your prospect while these sales questions, objections, problems – whatever you want to call them – are hiding beneath the surface, all the while preventing your prospect from listening to your message in an un-biased way.

If they are going to come up, it is better to get them out earlier than later. The way to do this is to ask simple questions early in the sales process:

- Before your appointment
- Early in the questioning stage
- On the telephone while asking general qualifying questions

Here are a couple of questions to consider:

1. If we were not to do business together, what would be your biggest issue?
2. If there is one thing that would prevent you from participating in this program, what would that be?

Smart Thing #66

Discover potential sales resistance early.

Dumb Thing #67

Seeing price objections as a problem.

Prospects/customers want several things from their suppliers: fair price, quality products and services, and timely service. Consumer surveys say that most consumers want timely and responsive service first, quality products and services second, and low price third. It is vital to understand the difference between price, cost, and perceived value. Price is what people pay for what they buy. Cost is what they pay for what they buy, over time; in other words, the cost of doing it late, wrong, or not at all. Perceived value is what they want for the money they are paying.

Most consumers tell salespeople that what they want is low price, when what they really want is low cost. Now I know that many of you will take issue with this statement, but I only ask that you consider for a moment what you *as a consumer* want. Do you want the cheapest, or that which solves your problem or answers your need or desire?

People object to price when they feel that what you are asking them to pay is higher than their perceived value. Most poor salespeople, when they get price resistance, lower the price. Most of the time, it is not a price or cost issue, but one of too-low perceived value by the prospect.

The real sales pros focus on value – what the product or service does for the customer – and not price. They understand that price is an issue, but not the most important one. Price will always seem high when perceived value is low. It should therefore be obvious that you never want to introduce price too soon in the sales process – until you have had the opportunity to build value in the prospect's mind. If you have a price-only buyer (they are out there), you must decide if that business is worth it to you in the long run.

Smart Thing #67

Never accept price as the primary objection.

Dumb Thing #68

Fearing sales objections.

Objections by good prospects are not negative. They are a sign of interest, a buying signal, or a request for more information. Objections from poor prospects are their strategy for getting rid of you.

I would like you to think of sales objections as unanswered questions rather than sales resistance. In other words, what is the prospect really asking when they say things like:

- "The price is too high."
  Could they be asking, "Why should I pay this much?"

- "I am happy with our current supplier or vendor."
  Could they be asking, "What are the advantages of switching to your organization or your product or service?"

- "We are going to purchase this product from you, but we need to wait until the end of the month, next quarter, or next year."
  Could they be asking, "What are the advantages or benefits of doing this now rather than later"

- "We need to check with some other suppliers before we make our decision."
  Could they be asking, "How is your service or product better than your competitors?"

- "We really don't need this product."
  Could they be asking, "What problem does it solve or pain does it ease?"

Smart Thing #68

Develop proven techniques

for answering objections.

Dumb Thing #69

Projecting your personal biases.

The objection that you will tend to have the most difficulty answering successfully is the objection that is most consistent with your own value system. What do I mean by this?

If you are a price buyer, and your prospect objects to price, you will tend to accept their objection. If you are the type of buyer who tends to think decisions over before making a purchase, and your prospect says to you, "We need to think this over" – again, you will tend to go along with their objection as rational or making perfect sense (because that is the way you buy).

This simple act of accepting sales objections that resonate with you because you can relate to them is nothing more than projecting your personal attitudes into the sales process. You don't have the right to do this. Furthermore, it makes no sense to assume that just because a prospect says that the price is too high, they actually believe it or mean it.

People lie. People often don't know what they want or why. People often buy things that they don't need. Why? Who knows – they just do.

When you project your personal biases into the sales process, you are assuming that everyone who buys buys like you and for the same reasons. You are also assuming that when they don't buy for a reason that is similar to one of your reasons, it makes perfect sense.

This attitude sooner or later is going to cost you a lot of sales.

Smart Thing #69

Stay neutral during the sales process.

> **Dumb Thing #70**
>
> **Not asking for the business.**

A number of years ago, *Sales and Marketing* magazine did a survey; their research indicated that 60% of the time in a sales-closing situation, the salesperson failed to ask for the order.

People want to buy things, but often they don't want to make the decision to buy things. Why? They want a better life, a more successful business, or happier relationships, but they don't want to commit the money, time, or energy that will give them these things.

Consider this: During every sales presentation a sale is closed. Either you sell your product or service to the prospect or they sell you on why they don't need it, can't afford it, or don't need it now.

Why don't salespeople – after going through all the time, energy, and effort to present their product or service – ask for the business?

I have discovered that there are five main reasons:

1. They fear a "no" or rejection.
2. They feel that if they have done a good job presenting the product or service, the prospect will buy.
3. They don't know how to close the sale.
4. They don't have a closing strategy.
5. They never got control of the sales process from the beginning and they don't know how to get it at the end.

> **Smart Thing #70**
>
> **Ask for the order.**

Dumb Thing #71
Lacking a closing strategy.

Closing the sale is not an event. It is:

- Having effective prospecting skills
- Having a closing awareness or attitude
- Related to everything that you have done up to the final close
- Based on the ability to come from the customer's perspective
- Grounded in the ability to create a high level of trust

Attempting to close a sale without all of the above criteria is to invite a "no sale" result. Most poor prospects attempt to get the salesperson to move to the close quickly and then base their decision not to buy on price or some other stall tactic that most salespeople can't effectively handle. Therefore the entire sales process comes down to a nickel or some differential that you can't control.

Few salespeople have a "closing strategy" – a process that they follow with each and every sales opportunity. They ask a few questions, jump into the presentation (too soon, I might add), try and overcome any objections, and go for the close. The successful salespeople know the outcome long before they get to the end of this routine process and they do it by ensuring that each of the above steps is in place before they ask their closing question.

People generally don't like to make buying decisions. The primary reason is that they don't want to make a poor or wrong decision. For years, traditional sales closing methods asked people to make a decision. For example: Do you want it in green or red? (Alternative choice close). Do you want to use your pen or mine? (Action close) Can we write up an order now? (Direct close)

Each of these closing techniques, even though it can work, has two fundamental problems:

1. It asks the prospect to make a decision.
2. The average salesperson is uncomfortable using it.

You Call *That* Selling!

Since people don't like to make decisions, I suggest you stop asking them to. Here is a simple close that I have been using for over 30 years. Make the buying decision for the prospect, and ask them to agree with the decision you have made. It goes like this: "Let's do this, is that OK?" "Let's arrange for delivery on the 15th, is that OK?" "Let's get together on Thursday at 10 AM, is that OK?"

This close works for three reasons:

1. It gets a decision made, but the prospect doesn't have to make it. By agreeing with you, they, in essence, make the decision. I have found that people want to get decisions made, but don't want to make them.
2. It is common language. I guarantee in the next 2-3 days you will either say to someone or hear from someone, "Let's go to the movie, OK?" "Let's go out to dinner tonight, OK?"
3. It is easy to remember and use, and it gets the job done.

When you use this close, the prospect has only three options:

1. They can go along with both your decision for them and your recommendation.
2. They go along with your decision, but don't like your recommenddation. In both cases, you have a close.
3. They go along with neither your decision nor recommendation. No sale. However, using this with a qualified prospect gives you a 2-out-of-3 closing percentage.

If two people want to do business together, they won't let the details get in the way. If they don't want to do business, any detail will get in the way.

Tim Connor, CSP

> **Smart Thing #71**
> **Have a closing methodology**
> **that works and is repeatable.**

Dumb Thing #72

Advertising concessions.

Advertising your willingness to make a concession before you are asked to make one is insanity. What do I mean by this?

During the presentation, you make the statement that you can give the prospect a discount. They haven't asked for a discount. They may not need a discount, but let me ask you – DA – what have you now set up by making that statement? Again – DA – they are going to ask for a discount unless, of course, they are deaf. And then you act surprised!

How about this one:

Your price list says something like: *Suggested retail price.* Now I ask you, are you going to be surprised when the prospect asks for a price concession at the end of the sales presentation?

Every day millions of salespeople make off-hand remarks or casual statements that send the message to the prospect – loud and clear – that this price, these terms, this feature – whatever – is a negotiable item.

I urge you to carefully evaluate all of the statements you make while selling to see if you are advertising your willingness to make a concession later in the process. One way to do this is to look at your most frequent negotiating requests from prospects to see if there is anything you have done or said that may have set this in motion.

Smart Thing #72

Address concessions only when asked for.

Dumb Thing #73

Lacking a lost-sale strategy.

We all lose business – sales that are not closed, customers who decide to use a new supplier, businesses that no longer need our products or services, or any number of other valid reasons. You cannot sell everyone and you cannot keep customers for life. It is a myth, no matter what you may have heard or read. The key is to not lose them because of poor performance, poor quality, poor service, or poor sales skills.

Some salespeople, when they lose a sale or a customer, go into a variety of irrational emotional reactions: They blame someone or everyone, they make excuses, they sulk, they get angry, or they run and hide. Successful salespeople understand the ebb and flow of business and relationships. If you have good sales skills, a good product or service, a positive attitude, a good prospect – sooner or later you will sell them. Here are a few suggestions to use when you lose a sale:

1. Follow-up with a thank you note or letter for their time.
2. Follow up with an after-sales critique or evaluation.
3. Follow up with additional proof sources, i.e. testimonials, articles, etc.
4. Accept the fact that things, people, and businesses change.
5. Find out what your competitor did better than you to get the business.
6. Don't let it negatively affect your attitude. Keep at it.

This week's lost business can be next month's sale. This month's lost customer can become next year's home run. You will win some and you will lose some. You won't win them all and you won't lose them all. Just remember: Staying power over the long haul is much more beneficial than short-term quick success.

Smart Thing #73

Know how to save lost sales before they are lost.

> **Dumb Thing #74**
>
> **Lacking walk-away power.**

Sooner or later, you will have to walk away from a prospect or a client relationship that is no longer worth your time, energy, corporate resources, or willingness to continue. What are the characteristics that could contribute to this decision? Here are a few to think about:

1. The potential for additional business just isn't there.
2. The time, energy, or corporate resources to keep this sale or relationship active is no longer a wise investment.
3. You have lost control of the sales process.
4. Your intuition or gut tells you to "walk away" from this one.
5. The prospect's/client's only interest is in price and they are not concerned about service, quality, or your ability to help them solve problems or grow their business.

There are other reasons, but most will fall into the above five. Here are a few questions to consider:

1. Are you failing to walk away from any business that you feel you should?
2. Do you have inconsistent reasons for not walking away from some business?
3. Do you have a walk-away philosophy or strategy?
4. Do you have a successful sales strategy that you use consistently to keep the sales process alive and well when the prospect or client forces you into a walk-away position?

I am not advising giving up too soon, not using creative sales appeals, or terminating the sales process because you may be over your head. I am, however, suggesting that you have a walk-away philosophy and strategy that you can use as a template when the value of current business or potential business is in question.

> **Smart Thing #74**
>
> **Know when a prospect is not a prospect
> and walk away.**

Dumb Thing #75

Negotiating when you should be selling.

Effective negotiating is not a substitute for effective selling skills. Many salespeople believe that they need to be better negotiators, when what they really need is improved sales skills. Let's define the requirements for effective and successful selling:

1. Maintaining a positive outlook and an enthusiastic and passionate demeanor
2. Finding and identifying good prospects (those who have a need, desire, and sense of urgency for a solution to a problem that your product or service will give them)
3. Positioning your product or service in the mind of the prospect as the best possible solution for their available resources
4. Presenting the characteristics (features and customer benefits) of your product or service to the prospect in such a way that they easily see how these solutions will be achieved
5. Disarming any unspoken sales objections during this process and then asking for the business (That's called closing, folks, in case you are unfamiliar with the term.)
6. Servicing your clients to ensure repeat and referral business, as well as a satisfied customer
7. Maintaining effective and accurate sales records

Let's define negotiating. Negotiating begins where selling leaves off. It is finding those areas between the customer and the salesperson where there are differences or a need for compromise in:

1. Features (what they can or cannot live without)
2. Delivery terms (what they need and what you can give them)
3. Financial terms (again, what they need and what you can allow)

Negotiating is finding a way to reach a meeting point or common ground where you and your prospect can agree with each other's circumstances and still have a win/win/win relationship.

Smart Thing #75

Know when to sell and when to negotiate.

Chapter Five –
Time & Territory Management Dumb Things

You can't manage time. Time passes.

You can't use time in advance, store it up, use it twice, save it, use it again, speed it up, slow it down, or do anything with it. All you can do in a framework of passing time is: manage people, activities, attitudes, resources, decisions, problems, failures, successes, risks, money, and circumstances. Time management is a misnomer.

If you have a time-management problem, I would ask you another question. What, from the previous list, are you having a problem managing?

Salespeople who seem to get more done don't do it with more or less time. They are just better organized, more focused, or more effective using the time they have. Each of us gets 24 hours a day, 168 hours a week, 672 hours a month, and 8064 hours a year to work, play, learn, grow, travel, sleep, eat, and any number of other activities.

Why is it that some salespeople achieve more results than other people? They don't have more time. What they do have is better personal management skills. They have priorities, and they keep focused on them – whether it is spending time with grandchildren or putting together million-dollar deals.

I love to work, but I also want to have a life other than my work. It takes organization, commitment, and focus, and then anything is possible.

How are you doing? Do you have enough time for everything in your life that is important? Is any area of your life getting short-changed?

A simple task to determine where you are wasting time or not using your time effectively is to keep a record of how you use your time in hour blocks for a week. I guarantee if you do this, you will quickly determine where you need some schedule, activity, or priority modification. Got to go. I have to get to my next task.

> ### Dumb Thing #76
> ### Not being organized.

For the past several years, I have been surveying my sales audiences to determine how much time salespeople actually spend selling. Let me define what I mean by selling: the amount of time you spend in front of a prospect or customer or on the telephone selling them. This does not include:

- Travel time
- Meetings
- After-sales service
- Waiting time
- Problem solving
- Administrative responsibilities

I realize that all of the above are important and often required by either your boss or your client/prospect, and that they indirectly can contribute to satisfy a customer relationship, repeat business, and customer loyalty. Having said that, how much time do you think the typical salesperson spends selling (and that's what you get paid to do)? What do you think? 80%? 50%? 30%?

You may be surprised to find out (and please keep in mind that my research is very unscientific, but fairly consistent) that the actual amount of time salespeople spend selling averages 10-20% of their total work time! Now consider if you will: You are currently earning what you are earning, spending less (on the average) than 30% of your time selling. Imagine what could happen to your income if you could increase that to 50%? In other words, you would still be spending less than 60% of your time selling. How about only 10%? Could you increase your income by at least that? I'll bet you could, easily.

> ### Smart Thing #76
> ### Use your sales time wisely by planning everything.

> ## Dumb Thing #77
> ## Using technology as a crutch.

Many salespeople are relying too heavily on technology today as a sales tool to:

- Contact new prospects
- Maintain contact with current customers
- Handle after-sales service issues
- Cultivate relationships with customers

Although technology is a wonderful tool and has made it possible for salespeople to save time and stay in touch – it is at what cost? Relationships, especially sales relationships, are about people. People want and need human contact. An email tip is a wonderful way to stay in touch with my clients and prospects, but it will never replace a personal visit or telephone call.

How often have you sent an e mail vs. picking up the phone?

How often have you sent a fax vs. setting an appointment with a customer to discuss the issue?

YES – technology lets you get more done more easily and is often faster (I mean, I am sitting at my computer in my home-office with a glass of wine while I write this, and who knows where you are or what you will be doing when you read this). I love technology, but I also enjoy talking with my friends, visiting with clients, and getting to know people on a personal basis, face to face. Nothing can ever replace that – not the fastest computer, glitziest website, or smallest hand-held device.

Be careful not to assume that everyone is as technologically advanced or competent as you are.

> ## Smart Thing #77
> ## Don't let technology replace the human touch.

> ### Dumb Thing #78
> ### Losing focus.

An ongoing challenge for many salespeople is the ability to stay focused in the midst of personal turmoil.

Salespeople who cannot separate their personal life challenges from their career responsibilities generally resonate their problems in some non-verbal or emotional way.

When you cannot separate these personal issues from your career roles, you will tend to:

1. Reduce your positive state of mind, therefore impacting your success
2. Increase stress that will impact your health and ability to be creative
3. Send mixed communication messages to your prospect or customer
4. Lose the competitive edge
5. Negatively impact the ability to listen effectively and communicate with integrity

Here are a few steps to consider in order to separate the areas of your life. Do this so that one area will not have more control over another area than you choose to give it.

1. Focus on something positive rather than negative in the area of your life that concerns you.
2. Spend time before each call or appointment in relaxation and/or a short meditation period.
3. Focus on your long-term life goals and your progress when life throws you a curve.
4. Develop little routines or positive anchors when you are troubled.
5. Carry some personal physical reminder with you of what is positive in your life.

> ### Smart Thing #78
> ### Learn to compartmentalize your personal life and career.

Dumb Thing #79
Always getting ready to sell.

Selling today is easier in many ways, but it is also more difficult in other ways.

It is easier because of the internet, globalization, improved customer education and sophistication, better quality products and services, improved organizational management, and increased selling skills training.

It is more difficult because of the internet, globalization, improved customer education and sophistication, increased consumer choices, organizational down-sizing or restructuring, reduced layers of decision makers, time compression, organization turnover, and product life-cycles.

So, how is the salesperson of today to survive, succeed, or even excel? There are a number of actions that can and should be undertaken:

1. Develop positive sales rituals.
2. Develop emotional/psychological anchors that keep you focused.
3. Read some self-help material every day.
4. Study the competition.
5. Know your own products and services better than anyone.
6. Develop career advocates.
7. Become a positive resource for your prospects and clients.
8. Keep asking yourself: How can I do it better?
9. Network with people who can help you.
10. Develop strategic alliances in your career with people who can advance your career success.
11. Subscribe to and read publications that service your industry or the industries of your clients and/or prospects.
12. Become a problem creator for your clients rather than just a problem solver.

Smart Thing #79
Start. Act. Follow through.

Dumb Thing #80

Poor sales forecasting.

One of the activities management expects of salespeople is to provide bottom-up feedback in the area of sales forecasting. Unfortunately, many sales managers shove their sales forecasts down the throats of their sales staff due to the demands/expectations for sales increases of senior management.

Salespeople, if they are in touch with their customers' and/or prospects' needs, problems, budgets, changes, and competitive initiatives, are better equipped to forecast future sales results in their territory. In order to come up with numbers that are reflective of "the real world" and satisfy the demands of management, salespeople must understand the factors that impact their future sales results. Some of these are:

1. Present sales levels per customer/prospect
2. Future needs, concerns, desires of customers/prospects
3. Competitive activities in the sales territory
4. General market conditions
5. Quality of the relationship with their customers
6. New or future product/service opportunities
7. Whether the territory has potential or is a maintenance territory

There are many others, but these tend to determine the accuracy of any sales forecast, whether weekly, monthly, or yearly. The key premises to remember when forecasting are:

1. People buy when they are ready to buy – not when you need to sell.
2. Ignoring competitors' initiatives will ensure a lack of integrity in your results.
3. You can't make up for poor sales skills with extra effort or time.
4. Numbers pulled out of the air will haunt you later.

Smart Thing #80

Blend optimism with reality when forecasting.

Dumb Thing #81
Poor territory management.

Many salespeople will waste a great deal of time calling on poor prospects – trying to turn poor prospects into customers, or trying to close prospects that do not want or need what they are selling. One of the key characteristics in more effective territory management is doing a better job of qualifying prospects prior to giving them your time, energy, or corporate resources. Let's look at a few ways to better manage your resource of time and territory management.

1. Ask more effective questions earlier in the sales process.
2. Pay attention to answers to determine whether this is a good time to sell to this prospect.
3. Develop a customer profile to use as a template for your prospecting.
4. Spend more prospecting time getting referrals.
5. Develop strategic alliances to help you improve your prospecting results.
6. Plan your call activities early in the week, month, or day.
7. Don't give poor prospects more time than they deserve.
8. Develop a daily checklist of what you will need to be effective.
9. Get more of your prospects to visit your location, plant or office.
10 .Don't spend time giving presentations to non-decision makers.

Smart Thing #81
See your territory as
an abundant source of business.

Dumb Thing #82

Spending too much time on poor prospects.

It is impossible to sell every possible prospect. Poor salespeople have the philosophy, "If they will see me, I will see them." Successful salespeople know that some prospects are better prospects than others. They also know that every customer is also a prospect for additional business or referrals. They use a customer profile as a template for determining who is worthy of their time. They use this system to determine who is the best-qualified prospect they should see now. Poor salespeople try to turn poor prospects into customers. The pros don't have time for this kind of activity. They want to spend their limited selling time with only well-qualified prospects.

How do you know if you are wasting time on poor prospects? Ask yourself:

1. Is the sales process taking longer than usual with this prospect?
2. Do they tend to give me the run-around?
3. Is there no sense of urgency with this prospect?
4. Do they fail to return calls or respond to my initiatives?
5. Am I applying too much pressure to get this sale closed?
6. Does this prospect trust me?
7. Do I know their Dominant Emotional Buying Motives?
8. Am I trying to make my timetable their timetable?

There are only two reasons to spend time, resources, and energy on poor prospects:

1. You have nothing else to do.
2. You are failing.

And neither of these will contribute to increased sales or success.

Smart Thing #82
Use a prospect profile to decide
who is worthy of your time.

Chapter Six – Record Keeping Dumb Things

Have you ever experienced a sales slump? Or just not achieved the results that you believed you should have? If you have been selling for at least 2-3 years, I guarantee you have had some tough months or even a difficult and challenging sales year.

Success in selling requires many skills, attitudes, abilities, and personal values. When a salesperson experiences a down cycle in their success, it is impossible to look at just one single area of their approach to the sales process or their attitudes at any given time in order to determine where the cause of the problem is. For example, if you are having trouble closing sales, is it because you are poor at closing skills or could it be that you are trying to close poor prospects? If you are having trouble getting through to the key economic buyer or decision maker, is it because you don't know who they are or could it be that your low self-esteem prevents you from feeling confident or comfortable even calling on prospects at this level?

Determining where the problem is requires information, lots of accurate information about sales ratios, actual numbers, trends, and comparisons. It is difficult to take corrective action if you are not aware of what the cause of your problem is or what actions to take. Just working harder, longer hours, or continuing to repeat the same behaviors over and over again is not the answer. This approach will not solve your problem, but it will keep you busy. One of the common denominators (there are many) among top salespeople is their ruthless evaluation of activities, behaviors, results, and progress or lack of progress toward their goals. Most poor salespeople will tell you they don't have the time to keep complete and accurate sales activity and results records.

Many sales organizations and managers require regular call reports from their salespeople, but those reports are, in most cases, just sales busywork. They provide little, if any, value for the salesperson or the sales manager on where current or potential sales problems are or their causes.

Dumb Thing #83

Not keeping records.

Keeping accurate sales records does not have to be a time consuming or difficult task. All that is necessary is that you develop the discipline and form the habits necessary to ensure that you are always working from a position of knowledge and understanding and not one of ignorance and uncertainty. There are a variety of activities and results that you might want to consider tracking to ensure you know what is working and what isn't. Here are just a few of the items I recommend that you track each day, week, month, or year:

1. Your average sales volume or revenue per prospect
2. Your average amount of time from first contact to closed sale
3. The top five reasons why prospects don't buy from you
4. The average number of calls/appointments to close a sale
5. The average number of referrals from clients
6. The percentage of appointments to closed sales
7. The number of new prospects in your sales funnel each week, month
8. The percentage of time spent selling vs. after-sales service or in administrative tasks
9. The average number of new prospect presentations given per day, week, or month
10. Your average number of sales per week, month, and year
11. The average number of lost sales each week, month, and year

---

Smart Thing #83

Spend time every day writing down vital sales facts.

> **Dumb Thing #84**
> **Not evaluating your results.**

OK, so now you have created routine record keeping activities each day, week, month, and year. If you will devote just five minutes a day, thirty minutes a week, one hour a month, and a day at the end of each year, this time – if well spent – will guarantee that you are in touch with the reality of the relationship between your activities and results. I recommend you purchase two of my sales tools to give you more in-depth information on this subject: *Soft Sell* (book) and *The Sales Success Planner* (Yearly Planning Manual).

Once you have the records, it is now critical that you evaluate them honestly to determine where you need to make adjustments or modifications in your behavior, attitudes, or skills.

The vital statistics you are looking for are the ratios involved from the records you have maintained.

Here are a few examples. What is your ratio between:

- Sales to new customers and to repeat buyers?
- Prospecting telephone calls and appointments?
- Sales presentations and closed sales?
- Sales to referrals vs. cold calling or other methods of prospecting?

Now it's just a matter of asking yourself some hard questions such as:

- Why did your sales average increase/decrease in a week or month?
- Why did you lose more sales in June than July, etc?
- Why is the sales cycle time to close increasing?

> **Smart Thing #84**
> **Evaluate your results weekly**
> **in order to plot better methods.**

Dumb Thing #85

Not establishing benchmarks.

There is one way to ensure success in sales in the future and that is to reduce or eliminate the number of mistakes, poor decisions, and failures. Keep in mind that each of these can be very positive for the person who routinely examines their life decisions and actions. The problem is: most people don't.

The vast majority of salespeople just truck along not connecting today's issues or challenges with yesterday's poor judgment, choices, or actions. Establish benchmarks in your life to guide you consistently toward your goals. Benchmarks can give you a number of critical advantages as you move from one day to the next on your journey. Some of them are:

1. Accountability
2. Re-commitment
3. Re-evaluation
4. Proper direction
5. A measuring device
6. Renewed belief
7. Growing passion
8. A warning sign

A benchmark can be analogous to the road signs while driving on a long-distance vacation to an area you have never been. It can also be a warning signal that something is amiss. If you are not careful, you may never make it to your destination. Here are a few benchmarks to consider:

1. What are you going to do better this year to accelerate your progress?
2. What guidelines do you have in place to ensure you are heading in the right direction?
3. What records do you need to keep to ensure that you stay on track?
4. To whom can you give permission to hold you accountable?
5. Are you going to spend regular programmed time in reflection and re-evaluation?

I believe that regularly measuring activity to learn which activities generate the greatest degree of success with the least amount of pain and stress is one of the best ways to ensure that the time and effort you put into your career, business, or life will yield outstanding positive outcomes.

What we do not understand,
we do not possess.

Goethe

Smart Thing #85

Create guidelines as standards to measure your success.

> **Dumb Thing #86**
> **Failing to improve every day.**

Selling is getting more competitive every minute.

- There are more suppliers, offering more choices.
- There are more ways to purchase.
- There are higher consumer expectations.
- There is less consumer loyalty.
- There is increased difficulty getting to decision makers.
- There is more pressure from management to sell more at higher margins.
- There is technology that is driving everything faster and faster.
- There is more information available today about customers, competitors, and the marketplace than at any time in history.

So, what is today's professional salesperson to do? Quit? Hide? Play more golf? Jump ship to another industry, firm, or territory? Many have tried all of the above, but soon learn that you can't hide from the relentless advance of life, business, and the world. There is one thing you can and MUST do if you hope to survive, succeed, and prosper in this new world order. That is, spend increasing amounts of regular self-improvement time and energy on learning – not just more, but what is necessary for success, peace, balance, and lifestyle.

How much time do you spend in regular planned and focused learning? If it is not a priority in your life, you will soon discover that your competitors are stealing your business before you even know it. Don't risk it. Start today: reading, listening, attending seminars, and investing in yourself. I guarantee that over the next few years it will pay off more than you ever dreamed possible.

> **Smart Thing #86**
> **Spend time every day**
> **improving your skills and attitudes.**

Chapter Seven – After-sales Service

The mission for many of today's organizations is improved customer satisfaction and retention through better after-sales service.

There are many companies that have put real teeth and accountability into their employee training to ensure they get the consistent results they say they desire. Unfortunately, there are many more companies who have only given lip service to this customer-driven philosophy or approach.

At the end of this section I will share with you what I believe are the Twelve Laws of Effective After-sales Service. These concepts must be integrated into any sales culture, corporate philosophy, or program to ensure integrity between policies and procedures and customer perceptions and attitudes.

Effective after-sales service is not a slogan, advertising program, a button that everyone wears, or a banner touting, "We-Care Attitude". It is a mindset or attitude that penetrates every department of the organization. It is a philosophy that is understood and embraced by every employee, regardless of position, length of service, or responsibilities. It is consistent, regardless of the point in the week or month, market pressures, department or branch, current sales results, current cash flow, management philosophy of the day, or market position.

It is not a "program" that is funded for the short term, but a corporate lifestyle that is on-going, regardless of the whims of management, the fickleness of customers, or the dynamics of the marketplace.

What prevents organizations from building this consciousness into the fabric of its management team and employees?

1. If the corporate culture has been traditionally profit- and/or earnings-driven, then it will be difficult to shift gears to a customer-driven philosophy.
2. If communication is heavily weighted in a top-down direction, you can bet that it will take lots of time and follow-through to re-focus to a bottom-up style.

3. If the management style is closed, authoritative, and/or hierarchical, upper management will – unless totally and completely committed to changing the attitudes of the organization as a whole – generally abandon this new and challenging change in philosophy sooner or later.

4. If employees have too much on their plate, because your business style is to run "lean and mean," it will be difficult to consistently enforce the policies and procedures necessary to maintain the integrity of actions consistent with your stated objective of satisfied customers.

An effective after-sales service philosophy requires constant vigilance and dedication to see it through, regardless of how difficult it may be to maintain the integrity of your policies and procedures that directly or indirectly impact your customers and their expectations of your product or service and organization performance.

One way to determine the effectiveness of your after-sales service philosophy is to regularly solicit customer feedback in a variety of ways.

Now to what I promised above.

The Twelve Laws of Effective After-sales Service

Law #1: The customer is not always right. However, the goal is not to discredit, embarrass, belittle, or challenge them in a destructive way. What we need to do is discover the source or cause of their incorrect perceptions, beliefs, or attitudes. The next step is to determine if the organization has contributed significantly to these incorrect feelings or if their source is the competition, the marketplace, or their Uncle Harry.

Law #2. The customer is never always completely wrong. There is always some element of their perception that is a true reflection of reality as they see it. The customer can be a teacher for us if we will keep an open mind and receptive, neutral demeanor. They can mirror back to us where our advertising, distribution methods, pricing strategies, administrative policies, or marketing or sales methods need improvement, refinement, or a major overhaul.

Law #3. The customer deserves your best, regardless of the time of day, day of the week, or month of the year. Working late last night because it was your monthly inventory or your annual sales blowout should not become my problem as a customer. The fact that you just returned from a week on the road working trade shows – although I have empathy for you – is not my concern.

Law #4. The customer deserves your best regardless of your training, length of service, or any other prevailing corporate attitude. So you are 60 days away from retirement and just filling time, waiting to get behind the wheel of your RV. Or you are a brand new sales rep whining that manufacturing just doesn't understand. Or you are on the first week of the job and still can't master this new piece of equipment. Or you are overstocked on a particular item, so you cut back on stocking the items that I use regularly and ask me if I will accept a substitute. These and thousands of illustrations like them, if they become *my* problem, will cause me to seek out your competitor.

Law #5. Don't pass the buck. Whoever hears a problem owns the problem. How often have you been transferred several times before you finally get to the right person? Have you ever heard, "It's not my job, problem, or function"? Don't get defensive or upset when I bring you a concern or complaint. Accept the fact that the problem exists and help me get it solved.

Law #6. Don't be too busy for your customers and don't make it difficult for them to do business with you. How many times have you *as a customer* gotten the feeling that you are an interruption in an employee's day or workload? Have you as a customer ever been made to feel like you shouldn't be having a problem with a product or service, that it is your fault that the item broke? Don't treat *your* customers this way.

Law #7. Employee are customers, too. Every employee that ever does anything within an organization ultimately is doing it indirectly for the customer. That makes every employee an ambassador, spokesperson, or representative of the customer. When an employee fails to serve another employee in an effective or timely manner, sooner or later the customer will feel the repercussions.

Law #8. If you must use technology, make it user friendly. Within the past week, I have had five voice-mail systems hang up on me. When I called back to get a person, I had to spend several minutes of my valuable time wading through endless recorder dribble. I finally called another supplier.

Law #9. Say what you will do and do what you say. Follow through, keep your promises, honor your commitments, and keep me (your customer) informed of your progress. Customers will tend to be more understanding, patient, and tolerant if you communicate with them with integrity and in a timely manner.

Law #10. Be interested, care, and act like you are glad the customer is doing business with you. People like doing business with people who appreciate their business. People are willing to give more of their business and money to businesses that are friendly, accommodating, and interested. You show you care by having up-to-date product knowledge; knowing who does what in your organization so you don't have to keep me on hold for 10 minutes, while you try to find someone to solve my problem; and smiling, even if it hurts.

Law #11. Keep private things private. I am not interested in your personal problems or corporate politics. I do not have the time nor am I interested in hearing about who did what to whom and why in your organization. I don't want to know that you are looking for another job. Sharing private, confidential, or personal information – whether you are the CEO or receptionist – is in poor taste and unprofessional. It also makes me wonder how much of my business you also share with other customers or suppliers.

Law #12. Think ahead of the customer with a problem-solving attitude. To survive and prosper in this decade and this new century will require that organizations and their employees, all of them, think well ahead of their customers and their potential future desires, problems, and needs. It will be too late is you just wait for the customer to bring their problems to you or communicate to you their future desires or needs.

Dumb Thing #87

Lacking an effective follow-up process.

One of the techniques used to improve client relationships and sales results is to have an effective follow-up system or strategy on prospects and customers. The advantages of follow-up should be obvious, but for those of you who are not sure, here are a few:

1. Remember: out of sight – out of mind.
2. It sends the message that you are a professional.
3. It implies that you are in it (sales, the relationship) not just for the money.
4. It helps competitor-proof the business.
5. It makes you look better than your competitor.

So, when are some times to follow-up, and how? Here are just a few:

1. After a client/prospect visit: Thank them for their time.
2. After you have closed a sale: Thank them for the business.
3. After you have solved a problem for them: Ensure that they are satisfied.
4. After you have received a referral from them: Send or give a simple thank you
5. After you have made a commitment to them: Doing it (following through) shows you meant it.
6. After you have met them at a trade show....
7. After you have sent them sales material....
8. After you have received an inquiry....
9. After you have sent them to your website to do some research....

In summary, here are two general rules for when to follow-up:

1. After they have done anything for you
2. After you have done anything for them

An effective follow-up can be a telephone call, fax, email, letter, hand-written note, personal visit, or any combination of these.

Smart Thing #87

When in doubt – follow up.

Dumb Thing #88

Not watching trends.

Are you watching the trends so you can keep your customers informed about how business and economic trends may impact their business in the future? What are some of the trends you should be observing?

- Economic ones
- Market ones
- Technology ones
- Buyer perceptions
- Product evolution
- Service needs/expectations
- Buyer groups

I can tell you that over 75% of my business today and for the past 25 years has come from only five major industries – and I selected those industries in 1973. Was it luck? I am not that lucky. Was it brilliance? I am not that smart. No, it was research into what I believed at the time would be long-term trends. That decision years ago has permitted me to keep my business growing and my new sales acquisition costs to a minimum.

How did I do it? I still do it today. I read the books, articles, case studies – whatever I can get my hands on – by the futurists. Who are they? Here are a few of my favorites:

Marvin Cetron, Roger Herman, Carolyn Corbin, John Naisbitt, William Strauss, Willis Harman, Paul Kennedy, Daniel Burris, Joe Pine and Jim Gilmore, and William Bridges.

If you want to guarantee your future career or business success, then I recommend you read at least 2-3 of such books a year.

Smart Thing #88

Research trends that can impact your customers.

Dumb Thing #89

Not asking.

Once a customer has been sold, this is an excellent opportunity to develop the relationship into a real winning relationship. But you have to ask for it. What would you like to have from this new client or customer?

How about:

- Referrals
- A letter of testimony
- The right to use them as a reference
- Repeat business
- Third-party influence
- A strategic alliance

What else can you think of?

Loyal customers – if you have enough of them – are a very valuable asset that can springboard your career just as fast as unsatisfied customers – if you have enough of them – can cause your career to take a nose dive.

Learning to ask for what you want and deserve from your customers, due to your exceptional service, is not only professional and acceptable, but is often expected by your customers. In fact, not asking a customer for any of the above can send a negative signal that you don't care, don't trust them, respect them, or feel they can help you.

Smart Thing #89

Learn to ask for what you deserve because of your service.

Dumb Thing #90
Going only for the home runs.

Every now and then, salespeople hit a home run: They close a big deal. When this happens, you have the right to celebrate and pat yourself on the back for your patience, persistence, skill, and perseverance. Most salespeople, from time to time, no matter what you sell, have the opportunity or potential for a Big One. If you closed only these big sales from time to time and nothing else in between, you would most likely starve. Successful salespeople understand the concept of hitting singles and doubles while they are working on one of those biggies. Why? Because the big deals:

- Can take longer to close
- Generally require more work
- Can leave you with a big Lost Sale hangover if they don't close
- Require more corporate resources
- Can take time away from the routine activities of closing the smaller deals
- Require a higher level of skills due to the nature of your contact

The critical factor is maintaining balance in the mix of big deals and smaller ones you are working on. Yes, a $100,000 deal could represent 20% of your quota for the year, but it could also take 50% of your time. Five $20,000 deals will tend to close faster and get you to the same outcome. What is in your pipeline? A lot of big deals? A few big deals? Just smaller ones? Again, the key is in the mix. The formula I use is ten to one: ten smaller active prospects in my pipeline to every big prospect.

The secret is to get the sales closed and then cultivate the client for more business. I would much rather have a higher repeat-business ratio than a new-sale close ratio. This strategy is not meant to give you permission to not focus on generating new customers. You can't upgrade a current customer until you have sold them the first time.

Smart Thing #90
Establish the "right mix" of prospects
in your pipeline.

Tim Connor, CSP

> **Dumb Thing #91**
> **Not seeing current customers as prospects.**

Many salespeople treat customers or clients as one-time sales opportunities. When they have this limited view, they fail to achieve additional sales opportunities with these customers. Not only is a client a client, but a client is always a prospect for something more.

In order to gain these kinds of results, however, the salesperson must have a repeat-business mentality. One of my favorite sales concepts is: Make a sale and you'll make an income; sell a relationship and you'll make a fortune. Some of you may be thinking: "Tim, I am getting 100% of my client's business now; how can they be a prospect for more business?" There is more than one way to get more business from clients. They can also be a source of additional business:

- By giving you referrals
- By letting you use them as a reference
- By their willingness to network for you
- By their willingness to give you third-party influence.
- By introducing you to their friends or business associates

As you can see by the above list, there are many ways a client can help you get additional business – even if you already have 100% of their business, which is often unlikely. Don't underestimate the power of third-party influence to help you sell more in less time, with less energy, and less corporate resources. If your current customer is a resource for you, they can have a dramatic impact on your future sales success.

Remember, it is easier, less stressful, less time consuming, and often more fun to do more business with a present customer than it is to keep finding more new customers.

> **Smart Thing #91**
> **Use your customers to help increase your contacts and sales.**

Sales Quiz Answers

Keep in mind that the answers to several of the questions are subjective. In many cases, there is no right or wrong answer, only a best or better answer. This quiz is not designed to give you an in-depth explanation for each answer, but rather to stimulate your thinking. With this in mind, let's take a look at what – after over 40 years of selling and teaching people to sell worldwide – I believe some of the best answers are.

1. They talk too much. They give information before they get it.
2. It impacts every aspect of the sales process and sales relationship.
3. Characteristics or traits of a product or service.
4. What the features do for the customer.
5. The beginning of the customer relationship.
6. Positive necessary sales signals.
7. Read people, listen, and ask good questions.
8. The fear of rejection.
9. Ranking:
   1. Attitude management
   2. People skills
   3. Prospect qualifying
   4. Sales Skills
   5. Presentation skills
   6. Product knowledge
   7. Closing techniques
10. Want, need, like, desire, can afford, will benefit from.
11. Emotionally. Logically.
12. You need to tell them to sell them.
13. Ranking:
   1. Service
   2. Quality
   3. Convenience
   4. Good terms
   5. Product/service reliability
   6. Organization reputation
   7. Price
14. From a sales attitude standpoint: the beginning of the sales process. From a skill or strategic standpoint: when the prospect is ready to buy.
15. Being sold to.

16. Your current customer base; past customers; referrals.
17. They give you credibility and reduce buyer fears and mistrust.
18. Can (but not much and not for long).
19. All the time.
20. It depends on how badly the customer perceives of his or her need. Many times poor salespeople are able, with the help of good prospects, to make up for poor sales ability.
21. The one that is the most consistent with your own values or beliefs.
22. False.
23. False.
24. True.
25. False.
26. False.
27. Getting accurate information early in the sales process.
28. False.
29. False.
30. Least.
31. True and False. It depends on a number of factors.
32. False.
33. False.
34. False.
35. False.
36. False.
37. It depends on a number of factors.
38. Trust.
39. They help you see where improvement will be helpful or necessary to achieve greater sales success.
40. Can I trust you and believe you? Are you looking out for my best interests or your own?
41. Being a better on-going resource for your customers.
42. False.
43. It helps you spend time with only the best prospects.
44. It depends.
45. The prospect's office.
46. False.
47. Raise the perceived value.
48. True.
49. The ability to ask well-thought-out, timely, and intelligent questions, and then listen.
50. True.

Scoring:

50 correct answers	You should be giving the quiz.
45-50 correct answers	You are a real sales professional.
40-45 correct answers	There is hope for you yet.
35-40 correct answers	With luck, you may make it.
30-35 correct answers	You are losing a lot of business.
30 or less correct answers	You need help big-time – call me.

Tim Connor, CSP

It's Your Turn

Personal Skill and Attitude Assessment

If you haven't already done so, now would be a good time to do a little self-evaluation on where you could use some improvements in your skills or attitudes. Under *Dumb Things You Need to Improve or Change,* list those areas where you feel you could improve. Also rank each item's priority:

? Immediate (now)
? High (short term)
? Medium (next few months)
? Low (whenever you can get to it)

Make sure that as you prioritize these, you do it according to your need and not your comfort level.

Dumb Things You Need to Improve or Change

1. Attitudes

Priority

[   ] Dumb Thing -

Smart Thing to replace it -

[   ] Dumb Thing -

Smart Thing to replace it -

[   ] Dumb Thing -

Smart Thing to replace it -

Priority

☐ Dumb Thing -

Smart Thing to replace it -

☐ Dumb Thing -

Smart Thing to replace it -

☐ Dumb Thing -

Smart Thing to replace it -

☐ Dumb Thing -

Smart Thing to replace it -

☐ Dumb Thing -

Smart Thing to replace it -

☐ Dumb Thing -

Smart Thing to replace it -

☐ 10. Dumb Thing -

Smart Thing to replace it –

2. **Prospecting**

Priority

☐ Dumb Thing -

Smart Thing to replace it -

☐ Dumb Thing -

Smart Thing to replace it -

☐ Dumb Thing -

Smart Thing to replace it -

☐ Dumb Thing -

Smart Thing to replace it -

☐ Dumb Thing -

Smart Thing to replace it -

☐ Dumb Thing -

Smart Thing to replace it –

Priority

☐ Dumb Thing -

Smart Thing to replace it -

☐ Dumb Thing -

Smart Thing to replace it -

☐ Dumb Thing -

Smart Thing to replace it -

☐ Dumb Thing -

Smart Thing to replace it -

3. **Sales Presentation**

☐ Dumb Thing -

Smart Thing to replace it –

☐ Dumb Thing -

Smart Thing to replace it -

<u>*Priority*</u>

☐ Dumb Thing -

Smart Thing to replace it -

☐ Dumb Thing -

Smart Thing to replace it -

☐ Dumb Thing -

Smart Thing to replace it -

☐ Dumb Thing -

Smart Thing to replace it -

☐ Dumb Thing -

Smart Thing to replace it -

☐ Dumb Thing -

Smart Thing to replace it –

☐ Dumb Thing -

Smart Thing to replace it -

Priority

☐ Dumb Thing -

Smart Thing to replace it -

4. **Handling Objections & Closing**

☐ Dumb Thing -

Smart Thing to replace it -

☐ Dumb Thing -

Smart Thing to replace it -

☐ Dumb Thing -

Smart Thing to replace it –

☐ Dumb Thing -

Smart Thing to replace it -

☐ Dumb Thing –

Smart Thing to replace it –

Priority

☐ Dumb Thing -

Smart Thing to replace it -

☐ Dumb Thing -

Smart Thing to replace it -

☐ Dumb Thing -

Smart Thing to replace it -

☐ Dumb Thing -

Smart Thing to replace it -

☐ Dumb Thing -

Smart Thing to replace it -

5 <u>Time & Territory Management</u>

Priority

| | Dumb Thing -

Smart Thing to replace it -

| | Dumb Thing -

Smart Thing to replace it -

| | Dumb Thing -

Smart Thing to replace it -

| | Dumb Thing -

Smart Thing to replace it -

| | Dumb Thing -

Smart Thing to replace it -

| | Dumb Thing -

Smart Thing to replace it –

☐ Dumb Thing -

Smart Thing to replace it -

6. <u>Record Keeping</u>

Priority

☐ Dumb Thing -

Smart Thing to replace it -

☐ Dumb Thing -

Smart Thing to replace it -

☐ Dumb Thing -

Smart Thing to replace it -

☐ Dumb Thing -

Smart Thing to replace it -

7. <u>After-Sales Service</u>

☐ Dumb Thing -

Smart Thing to replace it -

Priority

☐ Dumb Thing –

Smart Thing to replace it -

☐ Dumb Thing -

Smart Thing to replace it -

☐ Dumb Thing -

Smart Thing to replace it -

☐ Dumb Thing -

Smart Thing to replace it -

Personal Skill and Attitude Action Plan

OK, now that you know where some improvement is called for, it is time to move past the words and into the action. Knowing-and-not-doing is the same as not knowing. Why not use a rating system here, too? It will help ensure that you follow through. Rank each item's priority:

- ? Immediate (now)
- ? High (short term)
- ? Medium (next few months)
- ? Low (whenever you can get to it)

Make sure that as you prioritize these, you do it according to your need and not your comfort level.

Actions Areas for Development	Priority	Completion Date Goal

Summary

Here are the 15 biggest mistakes salespeople make:

1. They talk too much.

2. They give information before they get information.

3. They fail to observe and integrate early prospect signals.

4. They fail to effectively manage rejection and failure.

5. They sell when they should prospect, and prospect when they should sell.

6. They don't listen and take notes while the prospect is talking.

7. They inject their own values and/or buying prejudices into the sales process.

8. They don't effectively read buyer signals and act accordingly.

9. They sell features and price rather than value and customer benefits.

10. They don't keep good records or evaluate their wins and losses.

11. They don't work as hard to keep the business as they did to get it.

12. They don't ask for the business.

13. They focus on making the sale rather than selling the relationship.

14. They don't invest enough time and money in their self-development.

15. They confuse the importance of knowing with that of caring.

Now here are the traits of successful salespeople:

1. They manage their attitudes from inside-out instead of outside-in.

2. They are on fire with passion and desire.

3. They are a resource for their clients. They go the extra mile.

4. They are excellent communicators.

5. They are focused and concentrate on the task at hand.

6. They are able to win the support of all inside support staff.

7. They spend more time getting information than giving it.

8. They are masters at asking the right questions, in the right way, at the right time.

9. They sell value, not price. They know that, over time, this is the most important issue to the customer.

10. They manage their resources of time, corporate resources, money, and people.

11. They keep in touch with their clients on a regular basis.

12. Their primary goal is service and customer loyalty.

13. They honor their commitments.

14. They give something back to their community and their profession.

15. They are everywhere. They network and understand the value of good contacts.

16. They have lofty goals. They don't always reach them, but they aim for the stars.

17. They promise a lot and deliver more.

18. They understand the importance of knowledge of customers, competitors, and the marketplace.

19. Their word is their bond.

20. They work hard and smart.

Only in growth, reform, and change, paradoxically enough, is true security to be found.

Anne Morrow Lindbergh

Afterward:
Are salespeople becoming obsolete?

Will the continuous advances in technology replace the profession of selling in the foreseeable future? I am not a fortune teller or a mystic, but I do believe that we will see dramatic changes in the roles salespeople play in their organizations and the economy in general. During the next several years and stretching into the next few decades, there will be dramatic and all-encompassing change in every industry, field, and profession. No one will go untouched by the swath that will cut across every age group and discipline.

We are rapidly becoming a society that no longer talks to each other face to face. We communicate by fax machine, computer, email, answering machines, and voice mail. We are losing the human touch. I believe there are a number of reasons why the sales profession is alive and well and will continue to be so for years.

Here are ten reasons why salespeople will play a vital role in a growing economy. Salespeople are charged with any or all of the following:

1. They present new ideas, concepts, products, and services to current clients/customers and to potential clients/customers alike.
2. They assess the marketplace: i.e., customer satisfaction levels and perceptions, general market attitudes, competitor strengths and weaknesses, and consumer interest trends.
3. They witness and report on the emergence of grass-root market shifts and interests.
4. They soothe the ruffled egos of disappointed, frustrated, and/or angry customers.
5. They provide bottom-up feedback to the management of their organization on any number of opportunities, problems, and issues.
6. They are the front line of attack for any number of corporate marketing strategies and programs.
7. They work the trade show booths (a grueling task, if you have never done it) in thousands of trade shows each year.
8. They are on the look out for new product/service opportunities that a "corporate" person would never see.

9. They solve customer problems caused by poor design, poor pro-
duction, poor distribution, poor billing practices, etc.
10. They are ambassadors for management, building positive on-
going relationships that can increase business and profits.

I challenge you to find a computer, fax machine, software program,
customer service rep, or marketing person who can do all of this with
the courage of a mountain climber, the patience of a Job, the sacrifice
of a Mother Teresa, the energy of a two-year old, the creativity of a
Frank Lloyd Wright, the dedication of a mother, the wisdom of a
Confucius, the enthusiasm of a cheerleader, the commitment of an
Olympic athlete, and/or the persistence of a toddler.

The role of the sales professional will continue to undergo
transformation, but the fundamental mission will remain intact.

Index of Dumb Things

Attitudes

Prospecting

Sales presentation

Objections and closing

Time & territory management

Record keeping

After-sales service

Index of Smart Things

Attitudes

Prospecting

Sales presentation

Recommended Reading

Allen	As a Man Thinketh
Alessandra	Non-Manipulative Selling
Beaverbrook	The Three Keys to Success
Brooks	Niche Selling
Buford	Halftime
Conwell	Acres of Diamonds
Clason	Richest Man in Babylon
Connor	How to Sell More in Less Time
Connor	Sales Mastery
Connor	Soft Sell
Connor	The Ancient Scrolls
Connor	Win-Win Selling
Dudley	Earning What You Are Worth
Exton	Sales Leverage
Hill	Think and Grow Rich
Holtz	Winning Every Day
Johnson	Sales Magic
Jones	Life is Tremendous
Miller	Conceptual Selling
Meisenheimer	47 Ways to Sell Smarter
Meisenheimer	50 More Ways to Sell Smarter
Mortell	Anatomy of a Successful Salesman
Mandino	The Greatest Salesman in the World
Mandino	The Greatest Secret in the World
Marston	Emotions of Normal People
Peale	The Power of Positive Thinking
Ries and Trout	The 22 Immutable Laws of Marketing
Sobczak	Telephone Tips that Sell
Trisler	No Bull Selling
Winninger	Price Wars